The Politics of Down Syndrome

The Politics of Down Syndrome

Kieron Smith

zero books

Winchester, UK
Washington, USA

First published by Zero Books, 2011
Zero Books is an imprint of John Hunt Publishing Ltd., Laurel House, Station Approach, Alresford, Hants, SO24 9JH, UK
office1@o-books.net
www.o-books.com

For distributor details and how to order please visit the 'Ordering' section on our website.

ISBN: 978 1 84694 613 4

A CIP catalogue record for this book is available from the British Library.

Design: Stuart Davies

Printed and bound in the United States of America

CONTENTS

Introduction
My Kid Has More Chromosomes Than Your Kid 1

A Matter of Public Health 8

Education Policy 29

The Frankie Boyle Experience 46

The State Gets Personal 61

So What to Do About This? 70

References 73

PoliticsofDownSyndrome.com

Introduction

My kid has more chromosomes than your kid

There is very little written about the political role of Down syndrome (DS), and how it fits with the lives we live and the decisions we make about the way society is run. There are numerous medical and self-help titles, there is also a plentiful supply of books that address disability from an academic standpoint – this aims to be neither of those, but rather a political title that raises concerns about how the state and society treats people with Down syndrome and asks some questions about how, and why, this could change for the better.

I have had the great benefit of being helped with my understanding of society by my very beautiful five year old daughter who also happens to have Down syndrome. She has proved pretty much everything I ever heard about the condition wrong as she grows up. This is not a book about her, though she may have influenced me, and I own up to that now.

This is not a 'parent's book' of experiences, as I did not want to write a personal memoir about bringing her up. It is a book about a society that may or may not let her play a full part, may disenfranchise her and not let her fill her full potential. Many people never manage to feel they have lived a full and worthwhile life, and although of course I'd like her to, I'll be fine if she does not – not however if it is due to prejudice and ignorance that is standing in her way.

Worldwide, it is estimated that over 5.8 million people have Down syndrome. Down syndrome ignores any divisions of race, class or age. Approximately one in every 1,000 babies has Down syndrome; in the UK there is estimated to be 60,000 people living with the condition (Down's Syndrome Association) and in the US 400,000 (National Down Syndrome Society (NDSS)). In the US life expectancy for people with Down syndrome has increased dramatically; from only 25 in 1983 to 60 today (NDSS).

Society has come a long way in the last 20 years; we have for example seen the closure of long stay hospitals and move to care in the community, which saved many people with Down syndrome from the indignities of communal life. There have been considerable increases in medical knowledge about the syndrome, and there have been steps taken to include children with DS in education, when they were excluded entirely until the early 1970s.

Medical advances have meant that heart problems often synonymous with Down syndrome are far more easily corrected, (one of the reasons that life expectancy has been extended well into normal spans). Medical research also proving, that having an extra chromosome seems to protect against some forms of cancer. Having Down syndrome is not painful, and it certainly involves no suffering. Yet public health policy dictates the measurement of the 'risk' of bringing such people into the world at all, and permits termination, as a result, to the moment of birth itself.

I must underline here that in no way is this book anti-choice, I believe there should be a fundamental right for all women to have an abortion on demand. Rather part of this book examines a 'health policy' which takes women on a route to termination for Down syndrome which does not facilitate an informed decision.

Education has changed considerably and there have been some green shoots of inclusion since the 1970s. For many the experience has been mixed and many people with DS are still frequently denied effective access to mainstream education. Education as a whole has become more and more politicized and the way in which pupils with Special Educational Needs (SEN) have been treated, personally and by policy, has become tangled up with an emphasis on measurement and league tables.

Now we are in a position where the new coalition government in the UK talks of ending a 'bias towards inclusion', this is an opener to a debate that is likely to become very significant during the term of the administration. If schooling as a whole is to become remodeled and it's crucial that some pupils don't get left behind on the way.

Until very recently children with Down syndrome were thought to be unable to learn to read at all. Try to think about the world around you without using language, difficult isn't it? – We learn to interpret the world around us though language. People with Down syndrome have a very strong bias towards visual learning; something only discovered relatively recently. This bias is so pronounced that such people find learning speech and language very difficult indeed. Visual memory is good however and where language is lacking, reading may in fact be able to become a great way to help interpret the world.

This visual bias could be a boon in a society that has moved in that direction *en masse* – the internet, 3D films, video games and TV – we have transformed to being a society based primarily on visual stimulation and interaction. Often the best work open to people with Down syndrome is limiting, menial and banal, yet when given the resources people with DS show their talents as actors, photographers, artists, stained glass window makers, speakers, writers; expressing themselves in as many diverse ways as anyone else in society.

In this book I have used the term 'Down syndrome' often you will see it written as 'Down's' with an apostrophe 's' – this is more commonly used in the UK and the non-possessive used in the US. The term 'Down's syndrome' is what is called an eponym, where something derives its name from a person; in this case the physician John Langdon Down. I personally prefer the non-possessive spelling as it's not as if Langdon Down had or owned the syndrome and this type of eponym is falling out of use more generally.

In 1858 after graduating with his medical degree John Langdon Down joined the, then struggling, Earlswood Asylum for Idiots as its new 'superintendent' due to concerns from the Commissioners in Lunacy, after his appointment he reportedly set about improving conditions and treatment of residents. He left Earlswood in 1868 after a disagreement, despite some significant successes over his tenure. In the same year he founded, with his wife, Normansfield and started to take in residents, starting with 19 and growing to 160 in 1896 the year he died. The centre was to provide learning and care to the disabled children of the upper classes (Borsay 2005).

In 1866 whilst still at Earlswood John Langdon Down, a Victorian doctor of his time, identified what he believed to be particular racial characteristics in some of his patients. He then wrote an academic piece entitled *Observations on an Ethnic Classification of Idiots*. In his mind, and in the minds of many doctors well into the twentieth century, there was a distinct correlation between people's abilities and race, and there was perceived to be a hierarchy of races.

He wrote in his paper that: 'I have for some time had my attention directed to the possibility of making a classification of the feeble-minded, by arranging them around various ethnic standards' and goes on to give a survey of the various races he has witnessed in these idiots which are very different to 'the class from which they have sprung'. He continues to make the 'discovery' for which his name is still remembered today:

> A very large number of congenital idiots are typical Mongols. So marked is this, that when placed side by side, it is difficult to believe that the specimens compared are not children of the same parents. The number of idiots who arrange themselves around the Mongolian type is so great, and they

> present such a close resemblance to one another in mental power, that I shall describe an idiot member of this racial division, selected from the large number that have fallen under my observation.
>
> The hair is not black, as in the real Mongol, but of a brownish colour, straight and scanty. The face is flat and broad, and destitute of prominence. The cheeks are roundish, and extended laterally. The eyes are obliquely placed, and the internal canthi more than normally distant from one another. The palpebral fissure is very narrow.
>
> The forehead is wrinkled transversely from the constant assistance which the levatores palpebrarum derive from the occipito-frontalis muscle in the opening of the eyes. The lips are large and thick with transverse fissures. The tongue is long, thick, and is much roughened. The nose is small. The skin has a slight dirty yellowish tinge, and is deficient in elasticity, giving the appearance of being too large for the body. The boy's aspect is such that it is difficult to realize he is the child of Europeans, but so frequently are these characters presented, that there can be no doubt that these ethnic features are the result of degeneration.
>
> The Mongolian type of idiocy occurs in more than ten per cent. of the cases which are presented to me. They are always congenital idiots, and never result from accidents after uterine life.

Of course Dr Down saw degeneracy and racial characteristics because of the context he was operating in. Darwin's *Origin of Species* had been published only seven years earlier, and in some ways John Langdon Down's analysis was progressive, he finishes his article with the pronouncement: 'These examples of the result of degeneracy among mankind, appear to me to furnish some arguments in favour of the unity of the human species (Down, J.L.H. 1866).

He was of course totally wrong about degeneracy and racial characteristics, people with Down syndrome often have epicanthic folds on their eyes, and this was the primary 'characteristic' that enabled him to make his 'racial type' identification.

In Victorian times there was much to be made of the inferiority of races, and in 1866 Down was operating even before the height of British Imperialism. Generally this view continued well up until the Second World War when the Nazi's made such explicit genetic racism unpalatable to intellectuals.

Despite the out-dated and subsequently offensive meaning of the terms, the use of 'Mongolian Idiot', 'Mongolism' and 'Mongol' persisted until well into the 1960s. Most point to a complaint in 1965, when Mongolia approached the WHO about the use of the term, subsequently it was phased out, and we have been left with Dr Down's name.

There are recurring themes that we shall see in this book about prejudice, poor science, biological determinism (the idea that all we have inherited shall determine what we are to become, that there is a 'natural order of things' and we will all find our place, whether that be 'the rich man in his castle or the poor man at his gate') and who is deemed fit to exist in society and who isn't. Stephen Jay Gould in his excellent book *The Mismeasure of Man* writing on the nature of IQ testing and the idea of intelligence quotes: 'as Condorcet said [...]a long time ago: they "make nature herself an accomplice in the crime of political inequality"' (Gould, S.J.1984: 21).

Down syndrome is, rather than some form of racial degeneracy, a chromosomal disorder whereby someone has an extra (rather than the normal pair) Chromosome 21, hence it is sometimes called trisomy 21. This was only discovered in 1959 when Professor Jérome Lejeune proved that instead of 46 chromosomes usually present in each cell, Down syndrome has 47.

Yet long after the institutions have closed, and medical

knowledge has explained the nature of the chromosomal condition, we still live with the legacies of the Victorian era. Ghosts still live on in cultural echoes; of enforced regulation haircuts and shared ill-fitting clothing and group outings, leaving us with stereotypes that engender isolation and exclusion, of misunderstanding and stigmatization.

People with Down syndrome get very few chances to get their voices heard; there are a few notable exceptions to this; such as Anya Souza and Karen Gaffney. However Down syndrome, for reasons we'll explore in this book, is often dismissed because of what it is seen to represent, or glossed over as 'just a health condition' that's purely personal. I'll argue, contrary to this, that there are broader political issues to be taken into account, that by excluding some from society then all in society in fact are damaged, that inclusion is difficult, but essential, if we are to create a society that furthers human potential.

A Matter of Public Health

A few years ago members of medical research ethics committees in the UK were asked a series of questions about screening in pregnancy. They were asked whether it was ethical to screen for certain things with a view to treatment.

Look at the following list and decide for yourself whether you think it would be ethical or not to screen for:

(a) A life threatening condition (for neonatal treatment).
(b) Red hair and freckles (with a view to termination).
(c) A condition expected to reduce life expectancy by ten years (with a view to termination).
(d) A condition expected to reduce life expectancy by fifty years (with a view to termination).
(e) Slight lowering of educational potential (with a view to termination).
(f) Medium lowering of educational potential (with a view to termination).
(g) Severe learning difficulty, possible heart defects and slight reduction in life expectancy (with a view to termination).

Unsurprisingly most agreed that screening should happen for the condition described in (a); a very small number thought it was ethical to screen for red hair and freckles; most thought (c) unethical, (the person who wrote the survey had in mind type 2 diabetes for this). Opinion was divided on a condition that might reduce life expectancy by 50 years, in this case cystic fibrosis. Most thought screening for learning difficulties unethical and a majority objected to screening for (g) the description of Down syndrome in this survey (Archivist 2003: 607).

Prior to 2004 screening for Down syndrome was carried out,

focusing primarily on older mothers, those over 35, and those deemed 'high risk'. In 2003 the Labour government published a white paper entitled *Our Inheritance, Our Future – Realising the Potential of Genetics in the NHS*. In this it was asserted that 'Genetics knowledge will permeate healthcare bringing more accurate diagnosis, more personalised prediction of risk, new drugs and therapies [...] tailored according to a person's individual genetic profile'. It proceeded to promise that all pregnant women would be offered antenatal screening for Down syndrome by 2004/5.

This promise has come to fruition and it is now routine for women to receive these tests. Screening is presented in a matter of fact manner by the NHS:

> Screening tests can reassure you that your baby is likely to be born healthy, but can also prepare you if there is a chance your baby will be born with special needs. You do not have to have any screening tests if you do not wish to, although they can help your antenatal care team to provide the best care and support for you and your baby throughout your pregnancy (NHS 2010).

In reality very few expectant mothers decline the tests on offer.

These routine screening tests send a very strong signal from the very start, principally that Down syndrome is such a serious condition that a national screening program is necessary; which is the case in the UK and of many other Western countries. Most expectant parents believe that screening is compulsory and the NHS is seen as a caring service that people trust, so often are unaware that starting down this route can lead to an almost inevitable termination.

It is often insisted that screening is a matter of personal choice, yet there has been a concerted public health policy on Down syndrome (trisomy 21) unlike any other. Prospective parents are not offered a choice about potential screening options, for example to identify trisomy 13 (Patau syndrome) and trisomy 18 (Edwards syndrome). Indeed the 'genetic future' that the government identified in 2003 raises a number of challenges for society about what is, and is not acceptable in Public Health Policy.

In the UK there are very few things that are screened for during pregnancy. In the questions that proceeded this (d) the condition that could reduce life expectancy by 50 years (cystic fibrosis), which split the ethicists, could be screened for, as could fragile x, using similar techniques to those used to look for Down syndrome, yet we have no universal antenatal screening programs for these.

The UK National Screening Committee (UK NSC) recommends the following outcomes and benchmark time frames for the Down syndrome screening program in England: 'A detection rate (DR) of greater than 90% of affected pregnancies with a screen positive rate (SPR) of less than 2%. (Benchmark time frame: by April 2010)'.

In January 2009 *The Guardian* published a front page story claiming that a prenatal test for autism was on the horizon based upon the research being carried out by Professor Simon Baron-Cohen, director of the Autism Research Centre, Cambridge University. This story was later retracted as the research was not about prenatal screening. However the debate was an interesting one which exposed prejudices against Down syndrome and the implicit understanding that to screen was to screen out, Baron-Cohen was reported as saying:

> "If there was a prenatal test for autism, would this be desirable? What would we lose if children with autistic spectrum disorder were eliminated from the population?" he said. "We should start debating this. There is a test for Down's syndrome and that is legal and parents exercise their

> right to choose termination, but autism is often linked with talent. It is a different kind of condition" (Boseley, S. 2009).

At the moment there are three barriers that prevent higher diagnosis rates for Down syndrome prenatally. The first is that tests can become quite invasive and carry a risk to the fetus. Often non-invasive tests are described as 'the holy grail of prenatal diagnosis to try and find a reliable method of diagnosing Down's syndrome' (Professor Stephen Robson, spokesman for the Royal College of Obstetricians and Gynaecologists, in Wilkinson, E. 2010). Second is the low level of accuracy of non-invasive testing – only circa 75%. The third is that women do not always act as the policy dictates.

Medical 'holy grails' usually mean that there are large sums of money to be had, as do national screening programs. Consequently much more money has historically been invested globally on screening tests and their development than in ways to help people with the syndrome (Gibson 1978: 282). This area has also had its' share of minor financial scandals; with a US firm caught out over claims that it had developed a simple non-invasive test – which overvalued its shares, (which rose from $7.66 to $22.60 between June 2008 and January 2009):

> "You know it's definitely a Downs and you can read it [the test] as a Downs without any problem," she [Elizabeth Dragon, the company's vice president of research and development] said in a presentation in June 2008. But that wasn't true. The results showed success rates usually hovered around 70 to 80 percent, according to a Securities and Exchange Commission complaint (Tragester 2010).

The company's shares plunged 76 percent on the admission that the results had not been quite so clear cut (Armstrong 2010).

Down Syndrome Education International (Downsed), a

research based educational charity, has highlighted in their report *Wrongful Deaths and Rightful Lives* how public policy and medical professionals place such little value on the lives of people with Down syndrome that so many pregnancies are ended, where the fetus did not have Down syndrome, in the effort to positively identify the ones that do:

> Prenatal screening for Down syndrome affects millions of pregnancies every year worldwide. The vast majority of screen-positive results are false, yet encourage invasive diagnostic procedures that pose additional risks to unborn babies. As a direct consequence many babies who do not have Down syndrome are lost (Buckley, F. and Buckley, S. 2008: 79).

Screening is likely to become more effective with advances in genetic testing, and it is likely that a first trimester test, with low risk, could raise termination rates for Down syndrome higher than the already staggering 91% – figures also true of the USA, New Zealand, France and Singapore.

These termination rates and likely improvements of technique have prompted Brian G Skotko, from Children's Hospital Boston, writing in *Archives of Disease in Childhood* in 2009 to ask 'With new prenatal testing, will babies with Down syndrome slowly disappear?' He points to trends which show that the difference in expected births of babies with Down syndrome to be down 49% in the USA and 58% in the UK (Skotko 2009: 823).

Governments in the West, if not globally, over the last few years have taken a more and more interventionist approach to public health, welfare and the personal sphere. This has spanned everything from obesity through to parenting skills and exercise. In order to do this they offer 'support and information' to back up their own point of view. One social commentator has written that this 'support' is offered without being asked for and that '[i]n practice, it means placing pressure on people to adopt a course of action favored by government. Promote health by influencing people's attitudes to the choices they make' (Furedi 2005: 148).

This intervention into the public sphere is often couched in terms more familiar to liberation movements. Žižek identifies this as the 'post '68 spirit of capitalism' where troops enter Afghanistan defending women's rights and looking to promote emancipation (Žižek 2009: 58). This absorption of liberal rhetoric into an interventionist program is reflected in the views of mothers in the Netherlands (Skotko 2009: 824), who having terminated for Down syndrome believed that; 'DS was "an abnormality too severe" and a "burden" that was "too heavy" for the child'. Termination as liberation from learning difficulties suggests a particular managed approach to information provided to make an 'informed choice'.

I would, it should be said, defend a woman's choice to have an abortion as a fundamental right, this really should be an informed personal choice however and not something managed by government. In fact there is evidence that publicity around screening, improved tests and the routinization of this process can create greater compliance and a belief that there is no real choice in the process at all.

In 2007 the American College of Obstetrics and Gynecology (ACOG) took a stand against selection of fetuses based upon sex, they condoned this as potentially resulting in a society that could 'condone sexist values' (cited in Skotko 2009: 825) yet as Skotko asks has the ACOG's support for screening for Down syndrome not, by definition, 'endorsed a climate in which disability discrimination could more easily flourish?'

Cost benefit analysis

There is some enthusiasm for public health policies to be driven by economics; stop people smoking and you get a reduced lifetime cost of looking after the person by the state as a result. Not just in frugal times do governments have to grapple with rising public health costs and the challenge of improving a nation's health and keeping the books balanced.

In the West we have seen a steady increase in intervention by the state into the private sphere, whether it be through smoking bans, intervention on drinking, parenting etc. Moralizing and politics are often common bedfellows and in a more individualized and consumerist society perhaps it should not come as a huge surprise that government intervention on health is also often highly personal and moralistic.

Žižek pricks the internal nonsense in many of the health arguments promoted in his book *First as Tragedy, Then as Farce* where he finds himself in a hotel with a non-smoking policy put in place to 'guarantee that you will fully enjoy your stay [...] any infringement of this regulation, you will be charged $200'. He points out that 'this formulation, taken literally, is that you are to be punished for refusing to fully enjoy your stay' (Žižek 2009: 58). Public health policy seems much like this, in that it too is presented as formulated 'for your own good' and it's your moral imperative to believe this too, in the event you do not, then there will be repercussions.

In this case, it is the incredulity that you 'chose' to have a child with Down syndrome almost against the greater good, you have asked too much of society to support this child in any way and that you still expect some sort of equal treatment. One of the most common questions asked of new parents of children with DS is 'did you know?': 'One study indicated that obstetricians, the public and some geneticists were more prone to blame mothers of a Down's Syndrome child who had declined screening than mothers who were not offered it' (English, V. and Sommerville, A. 2002: 9).

There are many deeply held beliefs that inform this public policy, beliefs about difference, about population growth and a strong faith in statistics and science to provide answers to problems. In many ways if you believe that Down syndrome is a condition that is terrible then there is a moral imperative to screen against it, that this has positive effects in lowering later costs for intervention and support, also lowers the number of babies born each year and underlines the order of things too.

No personal views

In 2003 as the government's white paper was published there was a meeting of the International Down's Syndrome Screening Group in London. Prior to the meeting the organizers had been approached by some people with Down syndrome who had requested some time to talk to the conference, they were refused. Consequently they organized a demonstration in the grounds of Regents College, where it was being held, this then progressed to the main hall and the police were called. Before the police arrived however, the conference capitulated and let Anya Souza a woman with Down syndrome and a trustee of the Down's Syndrome Association, talk for ten minutes. She said:

> I can't get rid of my Down's. But you can't get rid of my happiness. You can't get rid of the happiness I give others, either. It's doctors that want to test pregnant women, and stop people like me being born (Adeline 2003).

A member of the International Down's Syndrome Screening Group's scientific committee, Professor Howard Cuckle, said that the attendees were talking about 'technical topics' and 'the conference was not the proper place for speakers to bring out personal matters' (Adeline 2003).

These personal matters seem only personal when they interfere with the allegedly personal choice to terminate. In July 2010 the Down's Syndrome Association published the results of a survey of new parents which found that 63% of mothers in the survey did not even recall being given information on Down syndrome prior to screening, although it is clearly laid out as a requirement in the National Institute for Clinical Excellence (NICE) guidelines.

Consumers?

When we look back at the early introduction of amniocentesis in detecting 'abnormalities' in pregnancy, which became widespread in the late 1970s and early 80s we see an interesting angle on testing. It was geneticists and 'consumer groups' who welcomed a ruling in 1979 from the New York Court of Appeals where doctors could be held liable for lifetime care if potential mothers were not properly advised and later bore a child 'with defects that could have been foreseen or detected' (*St Petersburg Times,* Florida).

Much of the twentieth century western capitalism was oriented around individual consumerist satisfaction – so why should having a baby be any different? Because Down syndrome effects all classes it was seen as different, and the birth of a baby with the syndrome especially for the middle classes can be seen as a challenge to fundamental beliefs, with resultant anxiety about 'community opinions, fear that the child will fail to achieve prescribed goals.' (Gibson 1978: 263)

Consumerism and choice were the touchstones of Regan and Thatcher's monetarist ideology and focus on the individual, a stance that politically did not really dissipate under the neo-cons in the new millennium. We still hear the echoes of Margaret Thatcher's now infamous interview where she talked about how society does not exist anymore:

> [People]are casting their problems on society and who is society? There is no such thing! There are individual men and women and there are families and no government can do anything except through people and people look to

themselves first.

Post-Thatcher it was as if there was implicit agreement that individuals rather than society did take precedence, however from the view of New Labour and the Neo-Cons there was a belief that the individual and personal sphere that remained could be guided by the state. Under the current UK Prime Minister, David Cameron, this is morphing into the idea of the 'Big Society' something where the state will still intervene early in family life but shirk its responsibilities to run schools or high quality healthcare. Cameron's vision of society is one 'where the leading force for progress is social responsibility, not state control' (The Conservative Party 2009).

A neighborhood army of five thousand volunteers, investment in charities and non-governmental social groups almost harks back to the nineteenth century where charity is there to provide schooling and address social problems, rather than have the state play the key role in addressing them. All of the Big Society vision still operates within the ideological boundaries of conservatism, which has often railed against the overweening state. The idea of the 'Big Society' and its language infers fairness and equal opportunity of access. Phillip Blond, a theorist close to the Cameron government, lays the blame at the door of the 'Big State' for failing communities, failing marriages, 'violence, poverty and dysfunction.' (Blond 2010: 283).

Although the 'Big Society' is still an emergent trend within the UK and to a degree the US (Obama's 'yes we can' focusing on society's collective responsibility), there is a feeling of *noblesse oblige* about a government 'empowering society'. For people to have responsibility and power – it has to be handed down from above. Consequently this could actually enforce hierarchical and a parent-child type relationship between the state and people.

Often in discussions about Down syndrome and choice there

is asserted the stereotypical view that the person will need constant support – that they will remain childlike throughout their lives. This view normally sees the child's parents dying and leaving the (now helpless) adult to the mercy of a cruel and unsupportive world. We all need some support during our lives, and people with DS are no different in that regard. However many adults with DS in this post-institution era are quite able to lead independent lives. The opposing objectivist view is incredibly narrow and ignores the significant support given by people to each other every day in society.

So where does that leave us?

The argument that termination decisions are made purely on a personal and private level fails to recognize that these choices also have a place within the society we live in. It would indeed be extreme to suggest that those facing a decision about abortion after a prenatal diagnosis had in their minds anything other than their own family and choices about their children. Yet their decisions cannot be taken out of context. There are several significant influencing factors that must be appreciated when considering these decisions, and the consequently high numbers of prospective parents who choose not to proceed.

The first of these is the role of testing in the first place. Screening for Down syndrome, since it was introduced, has been about screening out these pregnancies, with women being given a 'risk' level. The whole context is oriented towards making sure these babies aren't born.

Within the last ten years screening for Down syndrome has come to be offered as standard for all pregnancies:

> All pregnant women will be offered tests for Down's syndrome and every newborn baby will be screened for cystic fibrosis, under plans announced by the government yesterday at the start of a drive to promote policies on maternity [...]

> All pregnant women in England would be offered non-invasive tests for Down's syndrome, reducing unnecessary amniocentesis tests (Carvel 2001).

Frank Buckley, CEO of the research based charity Down Syndrome Education International, commented on screening:

> The 91% 'abortion rate' is on face value startling. However, it is virtually irrelevant as an indicator of parental choices. Indeed, it might be expected to be nearer 100%. The quoted rate is the proportion of parents choosing an abortion given a firm diagnosis. By this stage in the screening process, the parents have (1) chosen to opt into prenatal screening; (2) received a positive screening test result; and (3) chosen to accept an invasive diagnostic procedure that carries a 1%-2% chance of causing a miscarriage in order to obtain a firm diagnosis. It might be presumed that if the consent for the invasive diagnosis is 'informed' then it is based on the intention to abort given a firm diagnosis (Buckley 2008).

When a parent is given the results of a positive or 'high risk' test, often the next question to be asked is 'when shall I book you in for the termination?' The general limit of abortions to 24 weeks no longer applies, so although another fetus may be considered viable at 25 weeks, one with Down syndrome, by definition, is not. Dominic Lawson quotes one mother:

> I was told that my daughter had Down's when I was about 12 weeks pregnant and every doctor, gynaecologist I saw tried to convince me a termination was the best option. I was still offered this at 26 weeks! One reason given to me by a cold-hearted consultant was that 'these babies put a strain on the NHS' (Lawson 2008).

People have an understandable respect and trust of the medical establishment, if they are in an environment where they are being told that they should, in so many words, end this pregnancy then most will do so. Especially when we consider the further pressures being brought to bear upon them, many mothers are in a position of fear, and anxiety, consequently are vulnerable to the views of those in authority, whether the state or medics, and are unlikely to question what is perceived as 'standard practice'.

For some reason doctors and nurses have been laggards in their understanding of what it means to have Down syndrome and although there are significant exceptions to this, many have often seemed to have a very clear view of pregnancies where they consider the fetus to be disabled. There are also numerous stories of doctors regaling new parents with stories about how their new child will never walk, talk or using outdated or pejorative language.

Dominic Lawson writing in *The Independent* comments:

> make no mistake: despite all the progress which children with Down Syndrome are now making in schools and homes up and down the country, the medical profession in general still has a visceral bias in favour of eugenic termination, which its practitioners are often startlingly crude in expressing (Lawson 2008).

I suspect that this has some relation to the particular way in which Down syndrome was treated over the last century, and the lack of exposure that these professionals have had to developments in research. Even in our own experience from the diagnosis of our daughter, the pediatrician referred to people with Down syndrome as 'they' as in 'they enjoy physical activity' as if 'they' were somehow different to everyone else, and that having an additional chromosome created a set of interests to go with it.

As a result of this 'focus' on screening out Down syndrome many terminations happen where the incorrect diagnosis has been made: 'We estimate that current screening practice in England and Wales reduces annual live births of babies with Down syndrome by around 660 and leads to the losses of 400 babies without Down syndrome' (Buckley, F. and Buckley, S. 2008: 79).

In addition to the medical context of these decisions, parents exist in a world which as seen a dramatic politicization of the personal sphere over the last fifteen to twenty years. The state, the media and civil society have become increasingly involved, opinionated and interventionist in family life. This often treats parents, and adults generally, as if they themselves were still children, needing to be guided on the simplest of things, from the food their children eat ('fruit good, fat bad'), to how and when to read to your child. The resultant cocktail is one which Aldous Huxley would have recognized:

> Bokanovsky's Process is one of the major instruments of social stability!
>
> [...] Standard men and women; in uniform batches. The whole of a small factory staffed [...]
>
> "You really know where you are [...] Community. Identity. Stability [...] The principle of mass production at last applied to biology." (Huxley 1977: 23).

Huxley's dystopian vision was of course a manufactured one where human biology was actively managed, whereas the society we live in, has a more insidious cultural hegemony. This culture is one whereby the 'them and us' difference between the disabled and the rest of society is prevalent, and although there have been many moves towards physical inclusion, real integration is extremely rare. In most people's day to day lives they don't work or socialize alongside people with disabilities and this can only serve to strengthen this feeling of difference and 'otherness'.

Mums and Malthusianism

There is already a level of social stigma around women giving birth later in life, despite this becoming more and more common. There is a great deal of comment about being a burden on society and irresponsibility although recently this is starting to sound more resigned to the fact. Faced with the additional 'challenges' of a child with Down syndrome then 'older' parents understandably feel pressurized not to continue with the pregnancy. Often in discussions about parents who chose to continue the pregnancy – especially if they are older, you'll hear views on how 'it's okay now, but what will happen when the parents die, who will look after them (by then adult with Down syndrome) then?'

> One doctor said that women who delay having children until they are thirty-five or over constitute a 'major health issue', adding that they are more of a burden to society than teenage mums (Briscoe and Aldersey-Williams 2009: 12).

In the 1990s fertility rates shifted towards the thirty to thirty-five year old mother, from a previous average in the early twenties during the 1960s. This inevitably had an effect upon the likelihood of a diagnosis of Down syndrome in these pregnancies, as older mothers are more likely to have children with Down syndrome, although more babies with DS are born to younger mothers due to the greater number of babies born to this group in total.

Frank Buckley at Downsed has analyzed these figures and concludes that:

> Between 1989 and 2003, the percentage of all births in England and Wales to mothers aged 35 and over increased from 9% to

> 19%. It can be calculated that between 1992 and 2006, the natural (if no selected abortions) live birth rate rose 50% – from 14 in 10,000 to 22 in 10,000 [...] Meanwhile, the proportion of all diagnoses that were identified prenatally increased from 44% to 60%. Most (91%) pregnancies that are conclusively diagnosed are aborted (Buckley 2008).

So although there were more babies born with Down syndrome, the abortion rate also rose in parallel, due to the higher number of incidences of DS.

The other widely held belief is an extremely dangerous one. More and more it is accepted wisdom that the country and the world is overcrowded. That there are too many of us, more often too many of 'them' and something should be done about it. This Neo-Malthusianism is most commonly expressed in terms of an overcrowded country and calls for newer, tighter, immigration laws. This is not a massive surprise given the recent global recession and the resurgent rise in unemployment, where people often look to the person in the closest job to them. Malthusians always did have a view about what part of the population was growing too fast, and views about who should be curbed from reproducing, which of course did not include themselves.

More powerful than this view is the more recent link between the idea of over-population and environmentalism, where exponents of this idea applaud falling birth rates and back anyone who terminates, 'especially those with a disability'. This seems something of a jump, it is one thing to believe that this is an overcrowded planet and very much another to argue that abortions of those with disabilities is a positive thing. I believe this comes down to the concept of limited resources, that we'll soon be struggling to survive as a race on dwindling resource so, better that they are leveraged for the many than support those who would consume more.

One of the 'highest recommended' comments on a Guardian article online about screenings for Down syndrome, from a user called Roger Hicks, is representative of many;

> What disturbs me about this article is the presumption of "*moral superiority*" in those who oppose any form of eugenics. It is up to the individuals involved, of course, but aborting an unwanted child in our overpopulated country and world, especially if it is seriously disabled, is, in my view, a perfectly moral thing to do (comments on Shakespeare, T. 2008).

In actual fact the birth rate is declining in most western countries, and even 'high' estimates see Europe's population declining by 6% by 2050, 'low' ones as much as by 20% (UN figures quoted by Briscoe and Aldersey-Williams 2009: 12). Eugenics is such a loaded word I have tried to avoid its use, although it still has strong advocates. Hand in hand with the Malthusian belief that we can't cope with our rising population is the concern about *who exactly* this rising population is – and is it the right sort of people?

The *Bell Curve – Intelligence and Class Structure in American Life* was published in 1994 and for many remains a powerful, statistically packed, argument that there is a dangerous social trend whereby those with average and below average intelligence are reproducing more and having an effect on human IQ as a whole. The authors, Richard J. Herrnstein and Charles Murray, argued that 'it seems highly likely to us that both genes and the environment have something to do with racial differences'.

There is no explicit discussion in *The Bell Curve* of Down syndrome, and as people with Down syndrome rarely get the chance to have children, and babies with Down syndrome are born across what they define as the bell curve (they argue this is the normal spread of intelligence within society – the bulk of average people in the middle and smaller numbers at either end) then genes in our specific discussion appear unrelated. However implicit here is the lack of value placed upon those within the perceived lower end of a scale to measure intelligence and worth.

The lack of trust by the state in society, and consequently a belief in the importance of intervention into the private sphere shows itself in many ways. It's interesting to find research reports concerned about the low uptake of tests for Down syndrome amongst the lowest social classes, and the myriad of tactics suggested in the remedying of this situation (see for example Dormandy, E. et al. 2005). This also harks back to Malthusian concerns with the lowest social sphere's perceived lack of responsible reproductive behavior.

The authors courted a great deal of controversy, which we aren't going to run though again here, over their apparent assertion that race and intelligence are somehow linked. It is interesting to note however that this fallacy persists and gets intertwined with the prejudices surrounding learning difficulties and Down syndrome. There is an anti-human element to population politics and the politics of screening for a disability such as Down syndrome. Down syndrome is not a painful condition, people with it do not suffer, nor do they fail to add value to society. It's an idea we will return to, but at some point it happened that we started to screen out people with moderate learning difficulties. Down syndrome ended up in a perfect storm of institutional perceptions, the ability of society *to screen* and the willingness of the state to intervene on personal matters.

In addition to this the right to have an abortion has often been under siege. Consequently the Left could have been reluctant to take up issues which could aid the opposition (although the 'Left' has traditionally been very poor at engaging with the politics of disability in the UK). Disability activists raise the issue of screening, yet have achieved little traction primarily because of the lack of ideological coherency in any movement, and the diversity encompassed by the concept of 'disability'. Down syndrome groups themselves have on the most part also been unable to break through prejudice and the normalization of screening, in stark contrast to the media coverage on autism.

Public health policies should be scrutinized and approved by society, universal screening for Down syndrome has no positive mandate and no debate has ever been had. Out dated beliefs cannot be left informing policies which will affect more and more people as maternal age increases.

John Pearson

On the 28th June 1980 in Derby a baby, John Pearson, was born with Down syndrome. He had no significant complications; no heart or bowel issues often common at birth; he was not in any pain. His parents made the decision that they did not want him, and consequently the doctor, Dr Leonard Arthur, prescribed 'nursing care only' whereby he was administered only painkillers (a strong drug DF 118) to be administered 'as required' and water, but no nourishment. Dr Arthur recorded in John Person's notes that 'Parents do not wish baby to survive. Nursing care only'.

John Pearson was 'fed' water and DF 118 at regular intervals. By the evening the baby was 'quite blue in its extremities and its face was grey'. 'Feeding' proceeded every four hours even when he found it difficult to suck and frequently vomited. Born on the Saturday, by the Monday 'John Pearson could no longer feed from a bottle, so he was given water and pain-killer through a tube into his stomach. He was very restless and struggling to breath' (Kuhse and Singer 1987: 3). John Pearson died at 5.10am on Tuesday 1st July.

It appears clear that these actions were not unique and that this was not the first time that a baby with Down syndrome had been dealt with in such a manner. Rather than this time remaining private however a member of the hospital staff brought the case to the attention of the police and Dr Arthur was tried for attempted murder. Yet despite evidence that included that 'the level of DF 118 found in the liver of John Pearson was consistent with fatal poisoning' (Kuhse and Singer 1987: 3), the court found that it was the pneumonia rather than the pain killer that killed John, and despite the non-intervention of the medical staff to treat this, the doctor was acquitted. His acquittal principally based upon the combination of beliefs that firstly the baby's condition may have made him more susceptible to pneumonia, that 'nursing care' was normal practice and the administering of pain killers was more to give relief than to kill. During the trial there was a statement given by Sir Douglas Black, then President of the Royal College of Physicians, who said that: 'it would be ethical to put a rejected child upon a course of management that would end in its death [...] I say that it is ethical that a child suffering from Down's syndrome [...]should not survive' (Kuhse and Singer 1987: 8).

Kuhse and Singer write that this trial revealed that it was common practice to let handicapped infants die, and that this was 'endorsed by some of the most respected members of the medical community'. Jonathan Glover writing about the case in 1982 asserts that:

> A verdict of guilty would have been a morally undeserved calamity, an appallingly hard response to such a doctor trying in good faith to cope with a human disaster. The verdict was also welcomed on wider grounds. The hope was expressed that doctors faced with these decisions might now be free from additional worries about prosecution (Glover 1982).

Interestingly, at the time, the general public also seemed to agree. *The Times* carried the headline 'Women cry "Thank God" as Dr Arthur is cleared' and the BBC ran a poll which suggested that 86% agreed that a doctor should not be found guilty of murder if 'he sees to it that a severely handicapped baby dies' (Kuhse and Singer 1987: 10). Glover writes that 'In the long term, the problem Dr Arthur faced should become less common, because of antenatal screening'.

Education Policy

The most vulnerable children deserve the highest quality of care, so we will call a moratorium on the ideologically-driven closure of special schools. We need to end the bias towards the inclusion of children with special needs in mainstream schools.

Invitation to Join the Government – The Conservative Manifesto 2010.

We believe the most vulnerable children deserve the very highest quality of care. We will improve diagnostic assessment for schoolchildren, prevent the unnecessary closure of special schools, and remove the bias towards inclusion.

The Coalition – Our Programme for Government HM Government 2010.

Any adult in the UK with Down syndrome, who is over the age of 25 is unlikely to have been given access to any formal level of education. For those without special needs you would have to go back to 1870 for this to be the case with the introduction of the Elementary Education Act.

In 1944 The Education Act introduced by the Conservative R.A. Butler created a tiered system of education that deemed if children were 'educable' or not children with Down syndrome were considered 'ineducable', and consequently received no education at all. They were often consigned to institutions or, if they remained at home, possibly given some access to 'Junior Training Centres' where it was considered an almost charitable exercise to give some support to the 'educationally sub-normal'.

Things changed a little in 1971 with the White Paper 'Better Services for the Mentally Handicapped' which introduced segregated schooling based upon IQ measures: children with IQs below 50 were labeled as Educationally Subnormal (Severe)

– ESN (S) – and sent to schools established from the Junior Training Centres. Most children with Down syndrome were considered to have this IQ level as a result of their diagnosis; very few attended the schools for the Educationally Subnormal (Moderate), for children who were considered to have an IQ to 70.

It was only in the late 1970s that things began to change more significantly:

> Section 10 of the Education Act 1976, when implemented, will shift the emphasis of special educational provision within the framework in England and Wales significantly in the direction of greater integration and improved provision in ordinary schools (Department of Education and Science 1978).

In subsequent years there were green shoots of inclusion. However, despite a policy, resources were patchy. Much depended upon individual schools and what parents would fight for. Yet the right had been asserted and for at least a few children mainstream education became a reality.

Baroness Warnock, educated as a boarder at St Swithun's School, Winchester and then Oxford University was first asked to examine inclusion in schools for children with Special Educational Needs (SEN) by Margaret Thatcher, and the 'Warnock Report' is often cited as changing the policy of inclusion. However as quoted above, it was actually the 1976 Education Act that promoted the real change in policy. Warnock has for many years railed against inclusion and in 2005 wrote a pamphlet for the Philosophy of Education Society of Great Britain entitled *Special Educational Needs: A New Look*, where she further promoted the need for separate schooling for those children with SEN. We will return to the detail of her arguments in a moment as they are important and have had a significant ideological effect on the development of Conservative policy towards inclusion.

The experience of children with Down syndrome in mainstream schooling is mixed to say the least. Bob Black, the Education officer of the DSA says that 97% of pre-school families expect their child to go into mainstream, yet in 1988 when they carried out their survey of parents with children who have DS that about 87% of children with DS are educated in mainstream primary and about 23% transfer to mainstream secondary. Many of the children who do go to mainstream schools are held back in the reception year when their peers move up to year one.

To this day teacher training on SEN is basic:

> Although anyone training as a teacher has to show that they have an understanding of SEN, there is no requirement that they should have done any practical work with children whose abilities lie outside the mainstream [...] the government's chief adviser on discipline, Sir Alan Steer, warned that poor behaviour was being fuelled by teachers failing to identify pupils with SEN, instead labeling them "naughty" (Tickle 2009).

The experience of many parents is one of a battle – Brian Lamb who undertook the Lamb Inquiry published in December 2009, which looked into parental confidence in schooling described parents of children with SEN as some of the 'angriest in the country'(Tuckey 2010) (although he also said they were some of the happiest too – which isn't quoted so often).

The Lamb Inquiry successfully highlighted some of the key failures of the current system (as well of some of its achievements). Unfortunately it is now unlikely to hold much sway under the Con-Lib coalition. Under Labour, too, there was little apparent appetite to fully address the issues raised. The key message, alongside that of a greater voice for parents was that:

> The education system is living with a legacy of a time when children with SEN were seen as uneducable. Too often they are still set the least demanding challenges. We found many examples where disabled children and children with SEN were sidelined rather than challenged to be the best that they could possibly be (Lamb 2009: 2).

Children with DS have some very specific needs that can be addressed relatively easily in a mainstream setting – there is a crucial need for speech and language therapy, without which the child can find it difficult to communicate, interact with other children and form relationships.

Children with DS have, on the whole, a strong visual learning bias, and retain information far better this way than through verbal activities, so some tailoring of materials, visual timetables and an early focus on reading can provide access to a world that they are otherwise excluded from. It is difficult to process concepts and develop communication without language, so the written word can help massively in helping children develop. This learning strength is by no means exclusive to children with DS, so in a classroom setting others may well benefit from using similar visual tools.

Sadly for many, as they get increasingly frustrated by the lack of access to specialist therapy, there is a falling away from mainstream to Special Schools, where parents often feel that their child is given more comprehensive support. That said, although these schools may have a dedicated speech therapist, they are unlikely to have any particular specific expertise in Down syndrome. Additionally the environment is different, expectations may be lower and peers less likely to be able to help a child with DS model behavior or prepare them for the adult world.

In July 2010 the Children's Minister Sarah Teather announced that there would be a Green Paper on SEN in the autumn (now to be in 2011), after an Ofsted report on the same and in consultation with parents, teachers and interested organizations. She went on to say

> The system needs to be far more transparent. We need to give parents more choice and involve them in the decision-making process. The Green Paper will also look at how to manage the transition beyond school so that young people over 16 can get the support they need (Department for Education 2010).

During the election campaign David Cameron was confronted by a parent with his son over the Conservative manifesto statement:

> Mr Bartley tackled the Tory leader after he had delivered a speech on what he called the 'broken society'. He said "You are saying you want to reverse the bias towards the inclusion of children in mainstream schools. At the moment there is a bias against inclusion, not a bias for it, as your manifesto says." (BBC News 2010).

Cameron responded with the argument that he is in favour of parental choice.

So what can we expect from this Green Paper and where is education for Children with Down syndrome heading? There is very little on the subject in the Liberal Democrat Manifesto at all – they do assert that all five year olds will receive some form of SEN 'diagnostic assessment' and that teachers would receive improved SEN training. This is pretty weak so it was not a great surprise to see the Coalition Government statement on SEN revealed as virtually word for word that of the Conservative Manifesto (as quoted at the start of this section), it has removed the harsher sounding accusation of 'ideologically driven' though how either political view could not be this it remains to be seen.

The Conservatives have previously indicated that they would support 'independent assessments' of children with SEN, as their objective was to wrest the statementing power from the hands of the Local Education Authorities (LEAs). Education secretary Michael Gove was previously clear that they wished to use educational psychologists to create an individual 'Special Needs Profile' (SNP), whereby twelve or so 'support categories' would be reviewed and money would be allocated on a needs basis as a result (Tuckey 2010). This money would then be given to the school the child attends.

This view had been addressed previously since the SEN framework was established with schools being given greater autonomy over spending. In fact the Lamb Inquiry highlighted that there is a 'risk that some local authorities are too far removed from how services are being delivered' and that there was a 'failure to ensure specialist skills are accessible across all schools and to all children that require them'. Given that, and experience reflects this view even greater, deregulation suggests even greater challenges in ensuring standards and access for children with SEN.

Michael Gove has also had a strong effect on shaping educational policy, previously Chairman of Policy Exchange a right leaning think tank that actively promoted, as he has, the 'Swedish model' of free schools, whereby parents and teachers are given assistance and encouraged to establish their own schools. Gove, writing in *The Independent* in December 2008 asserted that 'Swedes decided to challenge declining standards by breaking the bureaucratic stranglehold over educational provision and welcome private providers into the state system' (Gove 2008). He claims that choice raises competition and therefore standards; a very free market model. However like most free markets it is not as free as it looks.

Policy Exchange published *A Guide to School Choice Reforms* in

March 2009 which examined the relative merits of Swedish free schools. These schools were expected to be more efficient than state run schools so survive on less central grant (75% of that received per pupil) – also, and importantly, these schools were not expected to accept pupils with 'serious special educational needs' (Meyland-Smith, D. and Evans, N. 2009: 24). There were also some concerns that companies looking to make a profit from these schools were excluding these pupils too.

The Policy Exchange publication also recognizes that although free schools often started out with 'one off' parent-led institutions, there soon emerged organizations running several schools and these became the more common experience. 'There is also evidence that schools in independent federations outperform 'one-off' free and charter schools' (Meyland-Smith, D. and Evans, N. 2009: 8). Inevitably and if they are to work then free schools need to be given some freedom so central government control is a challenge, and the policy has already attempted to push LEAs back from direct intervention; inevitably this could lead to inconsistency and complexity in attempting to ensure that there is equal entry and pupils are not unfairly excluded. So it makes sense that with the establishment of free schools with a per-pupil value of education that the exercise of working out how much it would cost to educate an equivalent child with SEN should be calculated.

There is a temptation, especially given the use of words such as 'ideologically driven' and 'bias' in the context of SEN and Special Needs Schools, to expect that there is likely to be a move of children with SEN to these (probably renamed) schools. Gove has already said that Heads of Special Needs Schools believed they could potentially provide more for the children than their counterparts could in mainstream 'and [be] significantly better suited to children's pastoral needs' (Tuckey 2010).

We will go on to look at how the Conservatives view SEN provision specifically, however there is an obvious issue here that free schools could well present more difficulties than mainstream state schools, for parents and children, in ensuring the correct expert level of teaching and support is available for pupils with Down syndrome. Free schools will not be expected to have to spend support money with LEA professionals for example, so measuring the effectiveness of any support provided will be difficult.

Conservative policy on SEN has been driven by their interim report group in 2005, established by the then shadow education secretary, David Cameron, and led by Sir Robert Balchin (described on the Conservative Home website as a key adviser to Margaret Thatcher and John Major, and as Chairman of the Grant Maintained Schools Council who 'did more than almost anyone else in those years to advance the cause of school freedom').

The submissions to this *Commission on Special Educational Needs* reflect parents frustrations with the process and its 'adversarial nature' the poor support in mainstream schools and the 'paucity' of special schools. The report states that

> many have made the point that their children are being made to suffer difficulties at schools because of the government's policy of 'inclusion' – how fair a representation of views this is difficult to judge as the submissions are not accessible and this suggests a common view amongst parents on policy rather than on their own individual experiences for their children (Balchin 2005).

Interestingly, the summary of submissions gives high prominence to two negative views from teachers and heads: firstly that 'their schools may be named on a 'statement' and they are then obliged to take a pupil for whom they can offer little or no appropriate provision'; secondly 'the presence in mainstream classrooms of large numbers of adult assistants in support of special needs children can distort the education of mainstream pupils.'

The report's recommendations reflect the comments from Michael Gove, the development of SNP to replace statements assessed by independent assessors. The funding attracted by the assessment would enable the parents to 'negotiate for a place' at either a mainstream or special school. This suggests a possible significant power shift away from the parent in the choice of school; currently the school named on a statement is compelled to accept the parent's choice.

In the summary the report emphasizes fairness, that the new approach be 'seen by parents as fairer'. The concept of 'fair' seems to be the new touchstone for the Coalition Government, the use of the word is telling and has recently been unpicked by *The Economist*:

> "Fairness" suits Britain's coalition government so well not just because its meanings are all positive, but also because – like views within the coalition – they are wide-ranging. To one lot of people, fairness means establishing the same rules for everybody, playing by them, and letting the best man win and the winner take all. To another, it means making sure that everybody gets equal shares. Those two meanings are not just different: they are opposite. They represent a choice that has to be made between freedom and equality ('Against Fairness' 2010: 13).

Much of the context for the discussion into the treatment of children with SEN in schools over the last few years has been set by Mary Warnock's 2005 pamphlet *Special Educational Needs – A New Look* (Warnock 2005), where she referred to the 'disastrous legacy of the 1978 Report, [being] the concept of inclusion' (Warnock 2010: 19). She promotes a double-think approach to inclusion whereby, it means completely the opposite, where a narrower use of statements provides a 'passport' to a newly reenergized special school system which could focus on 'Performing Arts or IT' (Warnock 2010: 14); and inclusion should be properly understood as 'being involved in the common enterprise of learning, rather than being necessarily under the same roof' (Warnock 2010: 32).

Warnock argues that students with SEN have suffered by being 'lumped together' as one group and included when their needs mean that it not always appropriate; also these children are often bullied and find large schools overwhelming. She writes that 'even if inclusion is an ideal for society in general, it may not always be an ideal for school' (Warnock 2010: 35).

Her argument appears to be that because inclusion is not working and children get bullied, they should be removed rather than the issues addressed. There is also an assumption that special schools would be able to address the needs that the mainstream schools would not – yet special schools have an approach which also often ignores specific research into particular needs. With Down syndrome, for example, research that now explains the need for early reading skills is not in common use, and although practitioners such as speech therapists are attached to schools they are generalists rather than offering the specific and specialist support needed.

In recent years there is some indication that parents who want the best for their children with DS may remove them to go to special school, with some confidence that at least the support they have been battling for will be there only to find that this too is lacking. Additionally that poor behavior of peers is modeled and expectations can be much lower than at mainstream. Unsurprising when these schools are seen as a 'last resort' for most, some with considerable practices, and staff with out of date views and experience – there are twice as many teachers over 50 in special schools than in mainstream (Tuckey 2010).

Only as recently as 2006, in the then Labour government response to a House of Commons Select Committee Report on

Special Educational Needs in the same year, was SEN training proposed as a core component to teacher training and the recognition that school SEN coordinators should be qualified teachers. Without the key skills and understanding of special needs, whether specific for children with a diagnosis as with Down syndrome or non-specific for many other children, whose special needs can be economic or learning bias in origin, then it is not a surprise that many teachers feel that children with SEN should not be included.

There is some evidence that many absolve responsibility to non-qualified teaching assistants and hold children back from progressing with their peer group because they do not have the skills or professional support to see learning difficulties as anything other than global delay. Richard Rieser blames teachers' unions and charities such as the Royal National Institute for the Blind and the Royal National Institute for the Deaf for the stalling of a policy of inclusion back in 2001 (*The Guardian* 31 Jan 2006).

Brahm Norwich, Professor of Educational Psychology and SEN at the University of Exeter, points to a parting of policy and statements from the Labour government where in 2006 Lord Adonis, the Parliamentary Under Secretary, told the select committee that 'the government did not have a policy of inclusion that resulted in closing special schools' in direct contradiction to the 'Removing Barriers to Achievement' strategy from 2004 (Warnock 2010: 51). Warnock has been quoted as saying: 'I find it interesting, the subterranean way in which Labour is coming round to special schools' (Quarmby 2006). She also described things as getting 'far worse from 1988 onwards [...] (for children with SEN)[...] who [...] were not going to help the league tables' (Select Committee on Education and Skills Third Report 2006).

So we find ourselves with a broad consensus towards some form of segregation in schools from the politicians and teachers unions, and for reasons which appear to come down to the failure to integrate properly. Not addressing training, not providing resources appropriately and using knowledge about particular conditions strengths and weaknesses. If the use of the term 'ideological' was meant in a pejorative way to refer to inclusion then that criticism stands if it is to describe a great deal of experience by pupils with Down syndrome as being more ideological than practical.

Individual schools and individual teachers have made great progress in this area, often with specialist support from the DSA or Downsed and in co-operation with parents. Once assumptions have been overcome then many schools have found inclusion is beneficial for the child with DS and the class as a whole. Teachers, when using their knowledge and making appropriate adjustments to the curriculum, have experienced a great deal of success.

One fantastic example is where a teacher, observing a worsening of behavior in a student with DS as he was not being intellectually challenged by the group he was in, moved him to the top math group where 'she was able to keep up to date with his progress and to encourage the use of peer support, which in turn, improved his social interaction' (Fox, Farrell and Davis 2004). This same study on effective inclusion (at primary level) highlighted that parents were very positive about inclusion and other pupils regarded their peers with DS in the same way they regarded any of their peers.

Warnock and other believe that progress made at primary school, where it has worked, cannot be replicated at secondary school where 'a Down's Syndrome girl [...] will now be excluded; her contemporaries having grown out of her reach' (Warnock 2010: 30). Given that we are continually letting down students with DS by not providing the best level of support, this final statement that their peers will just exclude them anyway, is both dismissive and patronizing to teenagers with and without

Down syndrome. It paints all children the same, some will be inclusive, some will not – but if we believe that a society of real fairness and equality is something we should strive for then we should do a bit of striving before declaring it a failure.

The Green Paper as well as drawing on these views is also likely to assert that we have the very concept of special educational needs wrong. This I believe will hinge on a few key points and justify a reintroduction of segregated education for those with learning difficulties. First off there will be an assertion that the numbers with real SEN has been far overstated; there is an oft repeated statistic that rather than there being the 2% of children who receive statements it is nearer 20% (Warnock 2007: 14) – this is a somewhat spurious statistic, there is no evidence that statementing is this high, is starting to lay the ground in articles such as that by Rosa Monckton, in *The Daily Mail* entitled 'It makes my blood boil that so many normal children are deemed to have special needs' (Monckton 2010). There is an element of truth that society has become too eager to look for medical explanations for children's learning problems (Furedi 2008); this however should not then justify an attack on inclusion.

The argument goes; there are too many children with spurious identifications of special needs, a proper independent assessment and then economic support for those who really require it, hand in hand with an understanding that there is no way that mainstream schools can really address their needs. Monckton writes firmly within these bounds:

> Let's take the dated dogma first, which boils down to a wrongheaded, one-size-fits-all belief that all children are equal and that, from the brightest to those with serious disadvantages, they should be educated together.

As a consequence, many brilliant specialist schools have been forced to close down – there isn't, for instance, a single school for mild learning difficulties like Domenica's [her daughter with Down syndrome] anywhere near our home in Sussex – and their hitherto happy pupils are bussed off to 'normal' schools all over the country (Monckton 2010).

Interesting use of language within Monckton's piece where 'special schools' become 'specialist schools' which are 'brilliant' and all these children with SEN being forced to integrate in what could be read as poorer schools because of 'our primary school teachers, still wedded to the out-dated, mixed ability, pupil-led teaching methods of the Seventies and Eighties'. *The Daily Telegraph* carried a piece by Francis Gilbert called 'Special needs is a fad that harms children' written from a different angle but much along the same lines, after discussing over-medicalization labeling of children with SEN as a get out for poor teaching and not addressing individual needs he concludes: 'All of which makes me think that perhaps it's time to junk the term "Special Educational Needs" altogether, along with much of the jargon that goes with it' (Gilbert 2010).

This attack on the more inclusive policy of the 1970s and 80s is likely to become commonplace over the next few years, where inclusion and differentiation are a poor fit with academy schooling. For corporations to look at running schools, they don't want to hear that 20% of pupils will need special attention and care, but if there are only *really* 2% who can be bussed back to 'specialist schools' well that's far more manageable.

There is an understandable concern about having a large number of children classed as having ADHD, dyslexia, autism, etc. and there has seemingly been a trend towards diagnosis as explanation for behavior or learning styles in many children (although the largest group still remains those who need extra support due to economic disadvantage). Fitzpatrick writes that: 'The enhanced prestige of people with learning difficulties and mental illness may reflect a lowering of horizons and a reduction of expectations, not only within the education system, but in society more broadly' (Fitzpatrick 2009: 35)

I could be persuaded that there may have been a lowering of horizons in society, although highly subjective, but to talk of 'enhanced prestige' even in respect to the advances on institutionalization, and for this to be at the expense of society's own development seems both nonsensical and reductionist in the extreme. The unfortunate logical conclusion could be that those with learning difficulties could in fact be *more* excluded if society were to demonstrate a more progressive agenda.

Warnock in her pamphlet quotes Alan Dyson who talks of a fundamental contradiction within the British educational system between 'an intention to treat all learners as essentially the same and an equal and opposite intention to treat them as different' (Warnock 2007: 14). This contradiction, it is argued, stops children with SEN receiving the specialist support they need. I have indeed argued similarly; that children with Down syndrome don't necessarily receive tailored teaching which takes advantage of the things we know about the syndrome, learning bias etc. However the logical conclusion it seems to me, is to make training of this available to mainstream schools so the curriculum can be differentiated in the right way.

Concerns here are that schools would; firstly, not be able to cope with the detail of what a child with a certain diagnosis has as strength or weakness, and secondly that by identifying (a medical) difference it works to be divisive. These arguments are spurious as teachers every day look at how to adapt to all pupils' learning biases and have a number of tools to allow them to do so; group and project work, now very common in schools, also works well to allow children to work together and support each other. Understanding the likely bias of a child with DS is not divisive in any way. It is more likely to assist with inclusion and hasten the learning curve of what works and what does not.

There is an assumption that special schools are equipped to

help children with their needs more appropriately. This is certainly not the case with Down syndrome: we have seen time and again evidence that special schools have neither the willingness to engage with up to date information on DS or the existing skills to properly educate children with SEN. For example courses run by leading edge research based charity Down Syndrome Education International are rarely attended by teachers from a specialist setting. Additionally a local charity which funds additional equipment for schools with children with DS found a marked distinction between special and mainstream schools, where the special schools were requesting things like light up balls and mainstream Numicon sets (a visual math aid) for the same age children.

Local Education Authorities (LEAs) are in an untenable position where they act as both the providers and funders of services which they are also tasked with constraining. As a result LEAs often allow statements to reflect what they can afford rather than what the child actually requires. A common issue for children with Down syndrome is the provision of speech therapy, which is both expensive and important, consequently resulting in frequent tribunals (also chaired by LEAs) where parents attempt to extract the correct level of support. The statementing process itself is also byzantine and complex, so is likely to expose a bias towards educated middle class parents willing to fight. That this system needs reform is not in question, the strengths of the system that should be retained (and developed) should include:

1. The legal requirement for a school to accept a child with SEN if their parents request it.
2. Currently LEAs allocate the funds that are spent to appropriate professionals, recognized speech therapists etc. making these funds freely available to spend by the schools on whatever support they deem necessary could

undermine consistency in professional support and understanding – which needs bolstering not undermining.

3. A collective and positive strategy for inclusion.
4. Compulsory training and experience for teachers in SEN.

Not everything is perfect in mainstream, this is clear, yet a move away from inclusion would be a retrograde step. There are many good teachers in mainstream schools who, given the right support, are able to take simple steps to achieve great inclusion to the benefit of all pupils and to the great advantage of the child with DS. As the Lamb Inquiry asserted one of the biggest issues facing the current system is that it is 'designed around the presumption of failure'.

The Frankie Boyle Experience

In April 2010 my wife and I went to watch a stand-up comedian called Frankie Boyle. Well known in the UK, Boyle has a reputation as a 'shock-jock' style comic. We had front row seats, not by design just that my wife books early for things she wants to attend. Boyle although 'shocking' is usually cleverly so, often challenging views which themselves are prejudiced or attempting to prick the bubble of celebrity and power. He has faced criticism for jokes about Israel's role in Palestine and cruel jokes about the Queen, and particular celebrities.

Boyle is not what you would call politically correct, yet he is actually someone who often jokes in a tradition which is progressive and clever, his methodology of pushing boundaries and intelligently confronting taboos. Humor, especially humor which challenges is difficult, as Carr and Greeves write, 'for a joke to give offence, offence must first be taken. Someone must hear the joke and respond to it with outrage' (Carr and Greeves 2007: 191).

Actually rather than 'outrage' we were sad and disappointed when Boyle told a series of jokes which targeted people with Down syndrome; we did not jump up, or intervene, just squirmed. My wife became upset, sad upset rather than angry upset, after Frankie Boyle went on about early death, bad clothes, elderly parents, using the word Mongoloid and even an attempt at a 'silly voice' pretending to be someone with DS who was largely incomprehensible. I leaned into my wife to ask if she was okay, and Frankie Boyle noticed, not surprising, given our front row position.

Upon asking what we were talking about, my wife told him our daughter has Down syndrome and she was upset, to this Frankie did pause and say that 'this could be the most excruciating moment of my career' and then proceeded to repeat that 'it's true though isn't it?' To which my wife and I both replied no, but did not want to continue our own excruciating moment. He said this was his last tour and he did not care anyway and tried to brush it off as part of his vicious humor.

It was not a great night out. The following morning in response to questions from her friends she posted a blog summarizing the evening before, describing how she felt. It was meant only for friends, but as these things do it got a little out of hand. After the blog was published it got circulated on Twitter and then started to gain momentum. Later that day she received a call from *The Guardian* who wrote a brief piece entitled 'Frankie Boyle meets his match in mother of Down's syndrome child' (Walker 2010). Over the next twenty-four hours things went a little mad with coverage in pretty much every national newspaper, television news coverage and BBC radio.

In the resultant whirlwind there were many misunderstandings; that we had stood up and confronted Boyle, that we had run to the press (and a fair amount of total nonsense too, including that we had *actually taken* our 5 year old daughter to the gig). There was quite a divided response from the public, understandably as many would know people with Down syndrome and find the jokes equally offensive, and many who believed we wanted to quash free speech and were *Daily Mail* readers who would be offended at anything.

> For the audience [...] the social rules are different and are further complicated by the fact that a great many of the individuals who take offence at a joke in a comedy show do so on behalf of a minority group of which they themselves are not members (Carr and Greeves 2007: 191).

In fact we were more just disappointed than offended, in a night out to face the same boring old prejudices about Down syndrome from a comedian who cites Noam Chomsky and

George Monbiot as influences; 'I got into Chomsky because I heard Bill Hicks talk about him in an interview. Bill Hicks is my favourite comedian and really was a political thinker in his own way' (Boyle 2010: 98). Something anti-progressive from someone who 'believes comedy is one of the last art-forms in which subversive, progressive ideas can be smuggled into the mainstream' (Dalton 2008).

We would still defend his right to use such material (many of the more right leaning papers were very keen for us to call on this 'to be banned'), but also retain our right to challenge it. Also for that matter our right to attend such a gig in the first place, something that seemed to be a common refrain for a few days 'parents of a disabled child should have known better than to go'.

Sharon wrote on her blog:

> So what was meant to be a great night out turned out to be a complete disaster. I don't feel that I did my daughter any justice at all. To the audience I was just 'some woman who got offended' […] And as for Frankie Boyle, well he has already told me he doesn't give a f*ck.
>
> I wish that I had managed to explain to them all why I was upset, to tell them how wrong the stereotypes about Down syndrome are. I wanted to show them how proud I am of my daughter, to tell them about how well she is doing at mainstream school. To show them the hundreds of pictures I have of her, so that they can see how pretty she is, that she wears pretty clothes and that she does not have bad hair (well apart from when she has put toothpaste or marmite in it anyway). I wanted to break through their prejudices and to show how wrong the stereotypes are. But instead all I did was make people think I was someone who couldn't appreciate live stand-up comedy. Which isn't the case at all (Smith 2010).

The story had started to morph into something else entirely, and has had surprising longevity – three months after the incident Julie Burchill wrote in *The Times* 'they were in the audience of Boyle's live show. And they confirmed that they were previously fans of the scumbag! Which pretty much made their complaint worthless' (Burchill 2010).

There are two fascinating aspects of this experience. Firstly, why did a comedian who, although 'offensive', professes to be progressive wander so far from this path and secondly why did it get so much discussion and attention?

The beginning of the 'skit' around Down syndrome started when Boyle selected a person from the audience and asked them what they did. Being in Reading, and near to the Microsoft 'campus' it was not a huge surprise that he had picked upon a Microsoft employee. At the time the Windows 7 campaign was running, with adverts extolling the benefits of the new operating system with the strapline of 'Windows 7 was my idea'. Boyle's joke was that the ad in his program was a picture of someone with Down syndrome saying Windows 7 was his idea (adding for no apparent reason that he had to make sure he found a model that was also dead).

There is a sort of middle class fear about Down syndrome, 'anxiety about community opinions, fear that the child will fail to achieve prescribed goals [...] as well as provide a pivot for whatever other family stresses are associated with middle-class striving' (Gibson 1978: 263). There was so much of the stereotype in what was said – both in the theatre and in the debates afterwards that Down syndrome started to appear to take a more general form of itself.

Boyle makes much of his 'clever' humor, for a working class boy 'made good' he prides himself on being literate and sharp. In this there is an archetype that emerges whereby the stereotype of Down syndrome represents something that Boyle uses to rail at. Not because it is a stereotype but because a stereotype is useful shorthand, something that conjures up the same image for everyone.

Susan Sontag wrote about how society mystifies illness and creates metaphors around them which greatly increases the suffering, by propagating beliefs about it being a punishment or curse. The most pernicious of these metaphors is cancer whereby 'cancer = death' (Sontag 1991: 100). She wanted to 'deprive something of meaning: to apply that quixotic, highly polemical strategy, 'against interpretation'' (Sontag 1991: 99).

Down syndrome seems to have transformed into a metaphor, a metaphor primarily for stupidity whereby words such as 'Mong', 'a Downs', 'Retard', are able to become an easy insult; a shared 'other' which represents idiocy and contempt. These terms, the images of institutionalization, represent a diminution of people with DS to something akin to sub-humanity. Where people with DS exist in a world where they remain forever dependent, forever children. This was also apparent in some of the coverage of the Boyle event: *The Daily Mail* in inimitable fashion referred to both 'Down's syndrome victims' and 'sufferers' (Loveys 2010), when the genetic condition creates neither suffering nor 'victims'.

The depersonalization of anyone with the syndrome by using the image created by the forced institutionalization of many people with DS – where shared clothes, haircuts and forced group activities seem a particularly cruel hangover from an era we are finally seeing the back of. In a society where the individual is king the worst possible position to be in is that of someone who cannot be an individual, who is forever consigned to a role of just 'a Downs', an 'other' to society.

When the Down's Syndrome Association responded to the Frankie Boyle incident they repeated a campaign they had used twenty-five years earlier; 'In 1985 we had a very successful nationwide poster campaign, with the strapline 'You say Mongol We say Down's syndrome His mates call him David'. However it seems that little of the essence has changed'.

For Frankie Boyle it is the metaphor that is useful, representing the stupid and the unengaged, the fear of creeping cretinism of uniformity and a life sapping dumbed-down culture. This has equivalence in his attacks on the banality he sees in celebrity culture. The problem is that it is a metaphor, but not just for Frankie Boyle but for all of society and it becomes an invidious one which increases exclusion and reaffirms prejudice.

Carr and Greeves write that; 'the urge to mock those who are disabled doesn't go away. We find their difference both threatening to the homogeneity of our community and useful as an anti-model against which we can reaffirm our normality' (Carr and Greeves 2007: 195).

Of course it would be wrong to assert that jokes about disability would be unacceptable, yet it is important to understand what we as a society find acceptable and what not, and why. A recent Ofcom study into offensive language found that the word 'retard' was polarizing, and that people found it unacceptable when directed at a group of people in a pejorative manor, this should not come as too much of a surprise, the people not offended contended that the word had changed meaning to be non-specific (Ofcom 2010).

There is a feeling from many that there are too many restrictions already on what is considered acceptable and what is not, Patrick West writing in *The Telegraph* represents this view when he writes:

> I do sympathise with the mother who went to see this self-hating Scotsman. I hope she appreciates that Frankie Boyle was not really being horrid about her daughter, but subconsciously pointing his anger towards an authoritarian culture which has as its favourite mantra: "You can't say that" (West 2010).

On this personal run-in with Boyle no one was saying he could not say the jokes he did, rather that the jokes he told were not funny; a legitimate criticism of any comedian.

Culturally Down syndrome finds itself in conflict with many of the trends of late capitalism. One of the most significant of these is anti-individualism, as we have touched on before. Fears of uniformity of being un-beautiful and outside of society, as an institutional-being; even for those people who have DS who have never been near an institution.

Minette Marrin writing in *The Times* asserts that abortion for Down syndrome is the best course of action as 'In a hyper-sexualised culture that worships bodily perfection, beauty and sexual success, adult life is also bound to be painful for people with Down's' (Marrin 2008). She also goes on to attest to a lifelong dependency on family and then social services. Support for people with DS will be necessary and some with the condition will need support in later life, but many will lead semi-independent lives. Not being an object of beauty to Marrin seems a particularly unconvincing argument for abortion.

Unfortunately even some parents of children with DS find themselves feeling pressure around the 'look' of the markers that DS often comes with. The condition has characteristics such as; a flat facial profile, flat nasal bridge, small nose, eyes that slant upwards and outwards, often skin that runs vertically between the lids at the inner corner of the eye (epicanthic fold), a small mouth which makes the tongue seem slightly large, a big space between the first and second toe (sandal gap), broad hands with short fingers and a little finger that curves inwards, the palm may have only one crease across it (palmar crease). (Seyman 2007).

The parents of one little girl in London gave her several operations when she was only five, one of these being: 'Folds of skin being removed from her eyelids to reduce the "Mongoloid" appearance traditionally associated with Down's syndrome'

(BBC News 1998). They did this to stop her being teased at school, although admitting that this had not being something she'd had to experience as yet. The mother was reported as saying: 'We live in a society that judges people by the way they look. Society is not going to change overnight so Georgia has to fit into society rather than society fitting into the way she is' (BBC News 1998). Given the quote from Marrin it's hard to disagree with the mother's view, she will indeed be judged, and will face prejudice, yet something feels wrong about resorting to plastic surgery for a child; surgery which will not change anything substantive about the condition.

Am I retarded or am I just overjoyed?

(Green Day *Jesus of Suburbia*)

It's as if the very idea the stereotype of someone who is 'retarded' is an antithesis to the cynicism and alienation of everyday life. If the first cultural stereotype is anti-individual the second is an attack based on the concept of the 'happy-idiot'; comments commonly made including 'they're [people with DS] happy aren't they'. People with DS have the same moods as anyone else, yet this idea persists and has the effect of underlying perceived isolation from a society that seems to actually crave a somewhat abstract sense of happiness and well-being (David Cameron for example has been a particularly keen advocate of this (BBC News 2006); and there are numerous books and TV series on the subject.

So to be perceived as 'being happy' despite the modern world is a point to underline otherness again, of not understanding or engaging with the world around you. Also if you are genetically happy then what need is there for others to feel a responsibility to their fellow human, to involve or care, consequently you can be easily dismissed. To be happy is also to be docile, unthreatening. Interestingly since the furor surrounding the Frankie Boyle jokes, although he never responded directly, he did tell a new joke about DS he was reported as making 'light of the upset he had caused, saying he had feared being 'hugged to death' by Down's syndrome children following the outcry' (Faulkner 2010).

This is a fascinating line and it shows the subtle nature of jokes whereby it plays on the shared understanding with the audience that people with DS are both harmless and happy, and that they might kill him – a juxtaposition that could be seen as positive, as it has the potential to challenge the perception.

Does the language we use about disability matter? I think the answer is probably yes and no. In these post-Politically Correct (PC) days we're probably through the worst excesses of muddling, changing the name of things as a substitute for actually addressing a prejudice or exclusion. It can only be fair if terms are pejorative and hurtful, to avoid using them. However change of language is not a replacement for real action or inclusion. In fact other words not even the epithets of 'Down's' or 'Mongol' in abstract really do the most damage – arguably the most significant piece of language that causes harm is the word 'risk'. When a pregnancy is scanned for the level of 'risk' of having a child with Down syndrome, rather than the chance. This word alone probably sends more of a message than any other.

The way in which Down syndrome is perceived, talked about and imagined has a direct correlation to societal pressures. Marshall McLuhan said all ignorance is deliberate (in our information rich environment) and with Down syndrome there are some very real and dangerous consequences of this ignorance. We have already discussed screening and education, add to that mix that at least one person appears in court every day charged with abusing someone with a disability (Equality and Human Rights Commission 2010). Additionally Mencap's *Death by Indifference* report found people with learning difficulties faced 'institutional discrimination within the NHS' which led to death and neglect.

In 1999 the Down's Syndrome Association carried out a major survey into attitudes of health professionals, entitled *He'll Never Join The Army*. This survey revealed extensive prejudice and active denial of access to appropriate medical care, they summarized:

> many medical staff view people with Down's syndrome as second class citizens and that these views often affect their treatment decisions. Other examples suggested that people with Down's syndrome had been denied routine treatment for common ailments such as hearing and sight problems, reducing their quality of life unnecessarily. In addition some parents with critically ill children were invited to withhold life-saving treatment, contrary to normal practice.

People do not suffer from Down syndrome, having an extra chromosome is not painful in the least, yet 'suffering from' is almost standard copy in the newspapers whenever covering a story that involves someone with the syndrome. This angle the 'victim' role of the person with DS sends the message that the condition should engender sympathy and charity, however it also sends the message that someone who needs help has failed.

There is what is called the 'social theory' of disability which, broadly, argues that it is society rather than the disability that disables people, I'm not arguing this is the case, people with Down syndrome do need additional support, however society significantly adds to the power discrepancy and undermines the equitable distribution of such support through negative imagery and emotive language. These can have very real and lasting effects on how people with Down syndrome are or aren't included in society.

The social model of disability has become almost a standard analysis over the last twenty years. Although sounding progressive, almost radical, it was adopted by everyone from social workers, governments and disabled groups themselves, yet it did not deliver what it promised. The result was a double-edged sword of a change in language that, although less discriminatory, was reductionist in nature whereby a word change *was the only change*. An individual with disabilities was now recognized as a person with distinctive needs but denied any actual assistance to play a full part in society.

We have already discussed how reproduction in society could be considered as having become more commoditized, Baudrillard pointed out the changed status of birth where society's obsession with genetic control and manipulation results in a desire for a 'clone-child' rather than a 'genuine other' – 'This is the child no longer in any sense as destiny, as the accident bearing death as well as jubilation for the parents, but the child as commodity' (Baudrillard 2002: 106). This commoditized child, also deprives us of our future as it represents something 'out of time' rather than the future, a technical process rather than one that creates our destiny. (Baudrillard 2002: 105).

There feels to be something of the prejudice against the 'other' in society's approach to children with Down syndrome. The unconnected nature of the birth of a child with DS, and the inability to link it to action or class, or race, its sheer universality makes it alien. The 'markers' which give children with DS some physical characteristics, such as blue eyes, and particular facial features only assist in highlighting difference and incongruity with parents and siblings.

This 'otherness' may have contributed to rejections by parents and a feeling, perhaps especially for the middle class, that this child was almost cuckoo like in its random and unheralded appearance. Previously I have discussed how genetic testing started at the same time as the consumerist, and individualistic environment of the late 70s and early 80s. We can see this in the extreme in a case in Victoria, Australia, where two women are suing their doctors for failing to diagnose DS in their unborn child, thereby denying them the chance to abort. *The Herald Sun* reports that; 'The couples are claiming unspecified damages for economic loss, continuing costs of care of the children, and "psychiatric injury"' (Betts 2010).

Emily

The image of the life of a person with Down syndrome as being in some way one of suffering and somehow 'unbearable' persists. In 2006 Siân Hughes, a little known poet, won the prestigious Arvon poetry award (previously won by Andrew Motion), for her poem 'The Send-Off' described as an 'elegy' for the 'Down syndrome child she decided not to have', she named her unborn baby Emily.

Hughes achieved a significant amount of coverage of her poem, many seeing it as a touching reflection of the difficult choice that the mother has to make. She appeared on Woman's Hour on BBC Radio 4 (2006), which received a fair amount of attention.

The Arvon poetry statement asserts that the poem has 26 stanzas reflecting the 26 chromosome pairings in a 'healthy child'; there is one extra line inserted in stanza 20, 'unbalancing the poem and echoing the child's diagnosis' (as a purely technical aside, this is incorrect – people have 23 pairs of chromosomes not 26 and the 'trisomy', the extra copy in Down syndrome, is chromosome 21, not 20 – the stanza where she inserts the extra line).

The poem shares the same title, 'The Send-Off, as the Wilfred Owen First World War poem, which she said in the Woman's Hour interview reflected a quiet understatement of the personal tragedy.

> somebody did some counting
> and when they added you up

> they found one part of you didn't match.
> It's supposed to come out even.
> They call it trisomy twenty-one.
> It's not such a lucky number.
> (Hughes 2009: 38)

Decisions on terminations *should* be personal and are always going to be deeply painful and distressing. Juliet Tizzard (Policy Manager of the Human Fertilisation and Embryology Authority (HFEA) – which, the Lib-Con government have announced will soon be disbanded, its regulatory powers dispersed to other groups) criticizes those who argue that the amount of choice in the decision whether or not to have a disabled child is due to imposed beliefs by society. She argues that this is no argument as consequently then 'no choice is made outside the influences of society' (Tizzard 2002: 37).

She has a healthy regard for parents' decision making and that they will be able to make rational personal decisions, including practical considerations about support, which if these pressures were removed and all were equal then 'for many prospective parents, the prospect of having a disabled child is not one that they consider best for them' (Tizzard 2002: 38). Tizzard rather undermines her argument by then repeating several myths around Down syndrome 'depending upon the severity of the condition' (Trisomy 21 is of course a chromosomal condition which you either have or you don't – there are not 'levels' of it).

In an ideal world Tizzard's position would be commendable, however to ignore environmental and economic factors, and pretend that prejudice and politics do not effect this sphere is naïve. For there to be real choice there must be a truly integrated society, one where people can actually interact with others who have conditions such as DS. To assert, as she does, that the economics of healthcare where screening is cheaper than lifetime support is just 'an unpleasant reality of healthcare provision' (Tizzard 2002: 40), sounds almost like it has tripped from the mouth of a Dickensian character.

Stigma

Erving Goffman wrote in the 1960s on the idea of stigma, of the 'abnormal' in society and their interactions with the 'normal'. He pointed out that our interactions with the 'abnormal' are intrinsically intertwined with stereotypes and that when this happens there is a danger that the stigmatized group can be perceived as 'less than human'. For people with Down syndrome stigma is extremely hard to circumvent due to the high visibility of the condition (also recall the parents who put their children with DS through plastic surgery); the fact that it is obvious that the person has the syndrome introduces 'uneasiness' (Goffman 1990: 66). This is then further hindered by the fact that many adults with DS have had poor speech so communication keeps underlining the difference.

In society the person considered 'abnormal' is expected to behave in a certain way, Goffman defines this as:

> The stigmatised individual is asked to act so as to imply neither that his burden is heavy nor that bearing it has made him different from us; at the same time he must keep himself at reasonable remove from us which ensures our painlessly being able to confirm this belief about him (Goffman 1990: 147).

The book exposes how people see the 'abnormality' and their interactions reflect this; in displaying rejection, 'over-hearty acceptance' or embarrassment (Goffman 1990). The book reveals people's surprise when they get to know the person with the stigma and discovering that they were, surprise, surprise, in fact just 'normal people too'.

I would argue that there still is a very real level of stigma around Down syndrome, and one, as we have seen very laden with stereotype. Goffman's book shows how this does not always have to be the case – One of his examples of a stigmatized group was homosexuals who, since the 1960s, have become far more integrated into society and suffer from far less stigmatization.

This stigma also has a new route in the internet which, visual in nature, can make easy prey of those with DS. 'Humorous' groups on Facebook that mockingly attack 'Downs' and 'retards', attacks on people with disability that are posted to YouTube as entertainment: 'The public has realised that those sites can be used to create virtual reality freakshows – and disabled people are being used to star in them, against their will (Quarmby 2010).

Recently there was a conviction of three Google executives for breach of privacy for failing to remove, after repeated requests, a video on YouTube of a boy with Down syndrome being kicked and punched in Italy; 'The footage was uploaded in September 2006 where it shot up to number one in the most viewed section and remained there for two months before finally being removed.' (Pisa 2010).

The internet is just a communication channel, albeit a powerful one, in these cases it just serves to underline the stigma borne by disability, and to some the legitimacy of treating those with Down syndrome as akin to non-human. There is no way to address the uploading of films or use of pejorative language; in fact any attempt to do this systematically is likely to curb legitimate freedoms. The only way to address prejudice and stigmatization is via familiarity and inclusion in society. The internet has also been a powerful force for progress in this area too connecting and informing, and through things such as *The Specials*; the recent Webby award-winning series about people with learning difficulties living independently.

The State gets Personal

The last quarter of the twentieth century and the beginning of the twenty-first has been a battleground between the personal and political spheres. The liberation movements of the 1960s and 1970s, both racial and sexual, proclaiming that the 'personal was political'. This originally positive assertion subsequently was absorbed into the rhetoric of the establishment and laid the grounds for an assault on personal behavior fuelled by distrust in people's ability to make decisions for them. This manifested itself in a series of moral panics including those around AIDS, child molesters and unruly teenagers and resulted in an unprecedented intervention into family life.

We can't be said to be post-intervention, although there is some definite softening of approach; backing away from ID Cards in the UK for example, and some of the more ridiculous child protection checks. After the last few years' experience however there is a strong temptation to balk at any further politicization of the personal:

> A child psychologist in Atlanta who terminated a Down syndrome fetus earlier this year said she was outraged by people who told her, "If you have to have a perfect baby, you shouldn't be a parent."
>
> "I was like, 'What!?'" said the psychologist, who is 35. "I've always been pro-choice, but now I'm pro-choice with a vengeance. Don't tell me I have to have a baby with Down syndrome just because you say so." (Harmon 2004).

This example is particularly apposite as the woman quoted uses the position of being pro-choice, itself a result of the feminist movement, in order to oppose the politicization of the legitimacy of the choice itself. However as we discussed previously, to dismiss the discussion of why people do make the choices they do is to not seriously address the issues surrounding Down syndrome, and need not be to the detriment of a woman's right to choose.

The idea of political correctness was the belief that because we have absorbed the language and position of liberation, that actual freedom has been achieved. We believed for society to change in the substantive that language was a crucial part. When figures came out of rising births with Down syndrome in 2008 (although incorrectly reported), the media covered it as increasing acceptance. In reality more terminations were happening than ever before and the percentage had risen. Yet culturally we cannot accept this about society, we believe ourselves to be more enlightened – it is a pity that the figures were not reported correctly, as the benefits of a society-wide debate on screening and acceptance would have been much more positive than a completely misguided self- congratulatory pat on the back for being more tolerant.

A risky business

The intervention in the private sphere and the focus on the individual through the ideological mashing of the 1960s and 1980s has effectively turned the world upside-down. Whereby the mass movements slogans emerge from the mouths of the political elite and the movements themselves are dispersed and atomized. In this new millennial society the 'progressive' liberal led states of the West are at risk not from the 'big threats' of the polarized Cold War, but rather the enemy on the corner of the street, the next door neighbor (who could be a terrorist or a pedophile), but fundamentally we are all turned in on each other.

Some commentators have seen considerable evidence of an emerging culture of risk and anxiety, where a 'growing sense of unease towards the informal sphere has shaped the way that individuals perceive the risks that confront them' (Furedi 2004:

81). Examples range from rape, to domestic violence, bullying and depression. This anxiety is likely to produce greater atomization, dependency on anti-depressants and lack of intimacy and trust.

A society struggling with a lack of faith in the human ability to change things, to successfully manage relationships and everyday life is also likely to find it hard to cope with the perceived 'risks' of having a child with Down syndrome. It's likely to conjure up a cascade of resultant personal risks too; the risk of splitting up over the child, of being trapped, of failing to provide for the child properly, of not coping.

If we become too obsessed with the personal then we lose sight of the political environment as a whole and the things which we share as a society. Sunny Taylor writes that people with disabilities are regarded as having 'suffered' some personal tragedy and that disability, because it comes in many forms, has hindered the development of a 'rights movement'. Consequently she argues that 'disability is a political issue not a personal one' (Taylor 2004: 91).

Back in the 1920s Crookshank wrote a book entitled '*The Mongol in our Midst*'. This was, as you might expect, a book of its time; it was a sort of perversion of Darwinian theory, claiming that 'Mongoloids' were 'among us' as either retarded or as those with 'dangerous cunning' who needed keeping an eye on. Obvious nonsense, Gibson describes it as

> a conspiratorial fantasy concerning the origins of the syndrome, along with supporting anecdotal evidence. His thesis was that DS is atavistic or racially regressive in origin and that only the more 'advanced' peoples suffer these genetic throw-backs (Gibson 1978: 71).

Our anti-human views of DS today are more finessed and subtle. Partially this is down to how we see value in people, often economic or financial; intrinsically a person's value in society is often perceived as how productive they are – catch 22 as on the most part people with DS are denied access to employment.

People with DS, although not explicitly nowadays, are often assumed to be of less value than others, we have seen this idea before whereby a life with DS was seen as a life not worth living and there were certain subjective judgments being made about what constitutes a valuable life. As well as economic value there is often a concept of independence.

The majority of adults with DS should be able to access a decent standard of independent living, and for those who cannot it does not mean in any way that this undermines value in life. Sunny Taylor writes that 'disabled people [...] define independence differently, seeing it as the ability to be in control of and make decisions about one's life, rather than doing things alone or without help' (Taylor 2004: 38. This sounds like a great description of independence to me.

Many adults post institutional care really appreciate even the most basic of human decisions; once you've been denied the right to make the choices about when to get up, when to go to bed what to eat and when these seem pretty great. A man with DS living independently, in his own home makes this point loud and clear; 'Soup for breakfast, now that's what I call independence!' (Newston, 2004: 141).

Humanity and the clear red line

Much of the recent debate about the nature of humanity has been around the ability to genetically intervene in the reproductive process. However this very soon starts to raise questions for all of us. *The Economist* leader raises the following dilemma:

> why deprive children of the chance to live without Parkinson's disease? But the queasy feeling takes over once parents start eradicating character traits such as homosexu-

> ality, or actively selecting good genes – athleticism, tallness, a high IQ (*The Economist* Editorial 2001).

Francis Fukuyama writing in his book *Our Posthuman Future* uses Nietzsche to good effect in highlighting what he sees as a 'clear red line around humanity', around all of us, appreciating that there is a rich tapestry of human life, ability and forms that we come in, but as soon as we start to chip away at this red line and redefine what constitutes humanity then there can be serious consequences for us all:

> The philosopher Friedrich Nietzsche was more clear-eyed than anyone else in understanding the consequences of modern natural science and the abandonment of the concept of human dignity. Nietzsche had the great insight to see that, on the one hand, once the clear red line around the whole of humanity could no longer be drawn, the way would be paved for a return to a much more hierarchical ordering of society (Fukuyama 1992: 155).

Much has been done to try and make this red line clearer. After the Second World War, international agreements tried to assert the

> basic rights and freedoms that everyone is entitled to, regardless of who they are. They are about how the State must treat you. They recognise that everyone is of equal value, has the right to make their own decisions and should be treated with fairness, dignity and respect.

The Universal Declaration of Human Rights of 1948 was closely followed in 1950 by the European Convention on Human Rights.

These were recently bolstered with the UN Convention on

the Rights of People with Disabilities, which was signed by the UK in 2007 and ratified on the 8th June 2009. The USA signed the convention on 30 July 2009 but has yet to ratify it.

The Convention has many interesting aspects, not least countries 'declarations and reservations'. Australia – long renowned amongst disabled groups for excluding immigration to the country based upon the migrant being likely to involve any extra cost to the Australian Community in medical or educational costs. Ironically in 2006 this included excluding a German doctor who was emigrating to the country to help relieve the lack of doctors in rural areas, who had a son with Down syndrome. The family was denied entry at every appeal stage, but was finally allowed entry after dispensation was given by the Immigration Minister (Foley 2008). Yet, still

> Australia [] declares its understanding that the Convention does not create a right for a person to enter or remain in a country of which he or she is not a national, nor impact on Australia's health requirements for non-nationals seeking to enter or remain in Australia, where these requirements are based on legitimate, objective and reasonable criteria.

The country still routinely excludes people with Down syndrome.

The UK also made a declaration which states that 'The United Kingdom Government is committed to continuing to develop an inclusive system where parents of disabled children have increasing access to mainstream schools and staff, which have the capacity to meet the needs of disabled children' (United Nations). Given this it will be interesting to see if this is fully abided by in the next few years.

Barack Obama signed the convention in July 2009. Importantly for people with Down syndrome the US has now signed into law the Prenatally and Postnatally Diagnosed

Conditions Awareness Act which requires those with a prenatal diagnosis of a disability to be provided with well-rounded information about the condition and also be put in contact with support groups and local networks,

> contact information regarding support services, including information hotlines specific to Down syndrome or other prenatally or postnatally diagnosed conditions, resource centers or clearinghouses, national and local peer support groups, and other education and support programs (cited in Buckley 2008).

The experience of parents in the US was very similar to those in other Western countries where the information presented to them was broadly negative (Skotko 2005). It is early days, fewer than two years has passed since the Act was signed, however it is a positive step.

So, how clear is our red line?

It is telling that disabled groups felt that although everything that enshrines the principles of equality already existed in the 1948 Human Rights Declaration, that there was still the need, 58 years later, to push for a Declaration to cover disability. That inclusion, dignity and equality still had not been achieved. That still in the most educated and advanced countries of the world, new legislation is needed to support the very fundamental rights that we should all be able to expect.

The key to this is a fatal misunderstanding. A belief that people are not actually equal, that we are born with differing abilities, and physical attributes. Some people are tall some are not, some can run fast, some are lucky enough, however it is appreciated, to have greater intelligence or creativity, etc. What should be inalienable because we are human, that we all should have equal opportunity, is actually not given as much credence in everyday life as we might like to believe.

Theodosius Dobzhansky, a Russian born geneticist, argued in a paper published in *Psychology Today* in 1973, that 'Differences are not Deficits'. He saw much evidence that even 'reputable scientists' still clung to the idea 'biology demonstrates that people are born unequal'. In a refreshing piece he draws out the very fundamental argument that is central to everything in this book. That equal opportunity in no way depends on an assertion that people are 'equal in endowment', and that 'a society of equality of opportunity is most propitious for human self-fulfillment' (Dobzhansky 1995: 631).

We are all unique, all have different genes, and in no way do these genes indicate our worth. 'Someone with a high IQ may be vicious, selfish, lazy and slovenly, while someone with a lower score may be kind, helpful, hard-working and responsible' (Dobzhansky 1995: 632). He uses IQ here yet adds the caveat that, and as we have discussed before, they are culture heavy and not free of bias. The fundamental point remains, that despite a natural trait that society places value on in abstract, it is not sufficient as a measure of anything.

There is a danger within equality of opportunity that we revert to the concept of things being 'fair' as we have discussed before ('Against Fairness' 2010). Opportunity is not equal to all in a society that is based upon wealth, class and education, so in some instances the very opposite can come about and socio-economic class can accentuate differences.

The hurdle for society is to somehow come to appreciate the essence of the title of Dobzhansky's work that *differences are not deficits*, that difference should just be accepted. This does not have to be divisive, it does not have to mean that difference is celebrated in a way that divides communities, and rather it should appreciate the commonality in the human experience. Because we are all different, our genes and experiences, then a society that recognizes and appreciates the talents and difference of everyone, is a society that can truly be both enlightened and progressive. Ignoring status, wealth and power and focusing on what each person can achieve.

So what to do about this?

I'm going to assume you agree on at least the general thrust of this book – that people with Down syndrome are given, on the most part, a pretty raw deal in society. Of course this isn't something exclusive to one syndrome, or one society: there are numerous other examples of stigma, exclusion, and inhuman treatment of others. Yet maybe if we start to extend inclusiveness, which I do not believe is something that is actually that break-through, which will open up debates about how we deal with everyone in society.

There is much being made of the return to a more social and trusting world, with both the US and UK governments expressing sentiments that inequality and rampant capitalism isn't the route to health and healthy countries. These views may well have been born of the last crisis, and are certainly part of the historical progression since the end of the Second World War. Books such as Wilkinson and Pickett's *The Spirit Level* are being lauded by the media and politicians of all hues, and extol the benefits of less distance between rich and poor, resulting in better life expectancy, education, lower crime rates, etc.

If we are to have a debate on the sort of society we want, on our desire to be more social, to have more trust, then it is an ideal time for society to engage in a debate on what society is and what it means to be human.

Over the last one hundred years, people with Down syndrome have been abused, eugenically planned away, denied access to education, to medical treatment, have had their human rights and voices ignored. Things have improved, and now is the time for more positive action to move further forward to a society where we could actually be proud to live. A society that has thought about and made rational decisions about how it treats people who happen to have different needs.

Proposals

1. No to Public Health Policy, not decided by the Public

Public Health screening with the express intent to remove people with Down syndrome from the population is divisive and a disproportionate response to both actual potential quality of life and exaggerates the health problems.

We are on the cusp of both non-invasive testing and the potential for testing for many other chromosomal and genetic disorders – there needs to be an open public debate about what these disorders really mean for those who have them.

Given that stereotypes and stigma often surround people with Down syndrome then this needs to be addressed not with imagery but by providing information to the public and expose people with DS as just being just as different and human as anyone else.

At no point should this be used to threaten a woman's right to choose to have an abortion.

2. A Bias Towards Inclusion

Education should be adaptable to help children learn. Children with Down syndrome have a specific learning profile, with an emphasis of visual learning, which once understood and adapted for is often beneficial to other children with the same bias.

Focus on central targets and lack of ability for schools to draw on effective professional support has created an environment pushing back against the green shoots of inclusion that started to emerge in the 1970s.

Inclusion should be a human right for children with DS and although it is recognized that schools should not be used as a tool for social engineering, neither should they contribute *in absentia* to the broader exclusion within society. No one reasonable would now argue that segregation should have continued in US schools between black and white.

Any attempts to re-establish segregation of the disabled should be opposed and affirmative action should be taken to include children with DS throughout their school careers.

3. Differences are not Deficits

Public engagement and challenges to beliefs on disability through 1. and 2. would do much to dispel some of the stigma attached to disability. It is recognized that changes to workplace inclusion, to stereotypes takes time Yet it is a journey we should as a society consciously embark upon because in the process we begin to value what makes us truly human. The consciousness of what we can do and achieve, of individual and collective action, of human progress.

The history of the twentieth century is filled with examples of how people were dehumanized and excluded; from pseudo-scientific IQ testing to extermination and institutionalization. Society in the twenty first century has the potential to build a new positive consensus, this could well be realized in the rejection of the distrust of difference and anxiety (about pretty much everything) with a new enlightenment of big ideas and achievement.

References

Adeline, P. (2003), 'Prenatal Screening: A Personal View', *Understanding Intellectual Disability and Health* [Online], Available at: http://www.intellectualdisability.info/diagnosis/prenatal-screening-a-personal-view [23 June 2010].

'Against Fairness' (2010), *The Economist*, vol. 396, no. 8689, July 3rd-9th 2010, p.13.

Altman, L.K. (1979), 'Ruling Stirs Debate on Prenatal Genetic Testing', *St Petersburg Times* 7 February 1979 [Online], Available: http://news.google.com/newspapers?id=wP0NAAAAIBAJ&sjid=PHwDAAAAIBAJ&pg=5341,4968825&dq=history+of+prenatal+genetic+testing&hl=en.

Archivist (2003) 'Ethics of antenatal screening for Down's syndrome', *Archives of Disease in Childhood* vol. 88, no.7, p.607.

Armstrong, D. (2010) 'SEC Says Ex-Official of San Diego's Sequenom Official Made False Claims', *Bloomburg* 3 June 2010 [Online], Available: http://www.bloomberg.com/news/2010-06-03/ex-sequenom-official-pleads-guilty-to-false-claims-on-down-syndrome-test.html.

Balchin (2005) *Interim report on SEN* London: The Conservative Party [Online], Available: http://www.conservatives.com/pdf/specialneeds-nov2005.pdf.

Barendregt, J.J. (2007) 'Economics and public health: an arranged marriage', *European Journal of Public Health*, vol.17, no. 2, pp.124.

Baudrillard, J. (2002) *Screened Out*, London: Verso.

BBC News (1998) 'Down's syndrome mother denies vanity' *BBC*

News 14 November 1998 [Online], Available: http://news.bbc.co.uk/1/hi/health/216479.stm.

BBC News (2006) 'Make people happier, says Cameron' *BBC News* 22 May 2006 [Online], Available: http://news.bbc.co.uk/1/hi/uk_politics/5003314.stm.

BBC News (2010) 'David Cameron tackled over special needs in schools' *BBC News* 27 April 2010 [Online], Available: http://www.bbc.co.uk/news/10088172.

BBC Women's Hour (2006) Interview with Siân Hughes, *Woman's Hour BBC Radio 4* [Online], Available: http://www.bbc.co.uk/radio4/womanshour/03/2006_48_fri.shtml.

Betts, M. (2010) 'Two couples suing doctors for failing to diagnose Down Syndrome' *Herald Sun* 21 July 2010 [Online], Available: http://www.heraldsun.com.au/news/national/two-couples-suing-doctors-for-failing-to-diagnose-down-syndrome/story-e6frf7l6-1225894802548.

Blond, P. (2010) *Red Tory, How Left and Right have Broken Britain and How We can Fix It* London: Faber and Faber.

Borsay, A. (2005) *Disability and Social Policy in Britain Since 1750, a History of Exclusion* Basingstoke: Palgrave MacMillan.

Boseley, S. (2009) 'Is autism screening close to reality? Call for ethics debate as tests in womb could allow termination of pregnancies', *The Guardian* 12 January 2009 [Online], Available: http://www.guardian.co.uk/lifeandstyle/2009/jan/12/autism-screening-health.

Boyle, F. (2010) *My Shit Life So Far*, London: HarperCollins Publishers.

Briscoe, S. and Aldersey-Williams, H. (2009) *Panic-ology, What's there to be afraid of?*, London: Penguin.

Brouwer, W Exel, J.V. Baal, P.V. and Polder, J. (2006) 'Economics and public health: engaged to be happily married!', *European Journal of Public Health*, vol.17, no. 2, pp.122-124.

Buckley, F. (2008) 'Informed Choices' *Frank Talk* 29 November 2008, [Online], Available: http://blogs.downsed.org/frank/2008/11/informed-choice.html [accessed 15 August 2010].

Buckley, F. and Buckley, S. (2008) 'Wrongful deaths and rightful lives – screening for Down syndrome', *Down Syndrome Research and Practice*, vol. 12, issue 2, October 2008 pp.79-86.

Burchill, J. (2010) 'Just how famous do you have to be to make it OK that you're a rapist or racist?' *The Independent* 14 July 2010 [Online], Available: http://www.independent.co.uk/opinion/columnists/julie-burchill/julie-burchill-just-how-famous-do-you-have-to-be-to-make-it-ok-that-youre-a-rapist-or-racist-2025993.html.

Carr, J and Greeves, L. (2007) *The Naked Jape, Uncovering the Hidden World of Jokes,* London: Penguin.

Carvel, J. (2001), 'Down's screening for all mothers-to-be', *The Guardian* 1 May 2001 [Online], Available: http://www.guardian.co.uk/society/2001/may/01/health.healthandwellbeing [accessed 15 August 2010].

Conservative Party (2010), *Invitation to Join the Government* – The Conservative Manifesto 2010 London: The Conservative Party.

Crookshank, F. G. (1925) *The Mongol in Our Midst: a study of man and his three faces,* New York: E.P. Dutton & Company.

Dalton, S. (2008) 'Is Frankie Boyle the UK's most shocking comic?' *The Times* 1 November 2008, [Online], Available: http://entertainment.timesonline.co.uk/tol/arts_and_entertainment/stage/comedy/article5037516.ece.

Department for Education, (2010) *Next steps on special educational needs and disabilities,* [Online], Available: http://www.education.gov.uk/news/news/sen-next-steps [accessed 7 July 2010].

Department of Education and Science, (1978) *Special Educational Needs: Report of the Committee of Enquiry into the Education of*

Handicapped Children and Young People, London: Department of Education and Science.

Department of Health, (2003) *Our Inheritance, Our Future, Realising the potential of genetics in the NHS* (summary), London: Department of Health.

Dobzhansky, T. (1995) 'Differences are not Deficits' in Jacoby, R. and Glauberman, N. (eds.) *The Bell Curve Debate, History, Documents, Opinions* New York: Random House Inc.

Dormandy, E. Michie, S. Hooper, R. and Marteau, T. (2005) 'Low uptake of prenatal screening for Down syndrome in minority ethnic groups and socially deprived groups: a reflection of women's attitudes or a failure to facilitate informed choices?' *International Journal of Epidemiology* Vol. 34, pp.346–352.

Down, J.L.H. (1866) Observations on an Ethnic Classifications of Idiots, *London Hospital Reports,* 3:1866, 259-262 [Online], Available:
http://th-hoffmann.eu/archiv/down/down.1866b.pdf.

Down's Syndrome Association, (1999) *Experiences of Inclusion, For children with Down's syndrome in the UK,* London: Down's Syndrome Association.

Down's Syndrome Association (1999) *"He'll never join the army" People with Down's Syndrome Denied Medical Care* London: Down's Syndrome Association.

Down's Syndrome Association (2004) *Access to Education, a report on the barriers to education for children with Down's syndrome* London: Down's Syndrome Association.

Editorial, (2001) 'Perfect?' *The Economist,* Apr 12th 2001 [Online], Available: http://www.economist.com/node/574049.

English, V. and Sommerville, A. (2002) 'Drawing the line: the need for balance', in Lee, E (ed.) *Debating Matters, where should we draw the line,* London: Hodder & Stoughton.

Faulkner, K. (2010) 'Frankie Boyle stuns audience with joke about Cumbria gun tragedy... just ONE DAY after 12 were shot dead' 11 June 2010 [Online], Available:

http://www.dailymail.co.uk/news/article-1285796/Frankie-Boyle-jokes-Cumbria-shootings-ONE-DAY-tragedy.html#ixzz0wnvlKWcD.

Fitzpatrick, M. (2009) *Defeating Autism, A damaging delusion*, Oxon: Routledge.

Foley, M (2008) 'Australia Relents in Down Syndrome Immigration Case' *New York Times*, 26 November 2008 [Online], Available: http://www.nytimes.com/2008/11/26/world/asia/27australia.html?_r=1.

Fox, S., Farrell, P. and Davis, P, (2004) 'Factors associated with the effective inclusion of primary aged pupils with Down's syndrome', *British Journal of Special Education*, vol. 31, no. 4, pp.184-190.

Fukuyama, F. (2002) *Our Posthuman Future, Consequences of the Biotechnology Revolution*, London: Profile Books.

Furedi, F (2004) *Therapy Culture, Cultivating vulnerability in an uncertain age*, London: Routledge.

Furedi, F. (2005) *Politics of Fear*, London: Continuum.

Furedi, F. (2008) *Paranoid Parenting, Why Ignoring the Experts May be Best for Your Child*, London: Continuum.

Gibson, D. (1978) *Down's Syndrome, the psychology of mongolism*, Cambridge: Cambridge University Press.

Gilbert, F. (2010), 'Special needs is a fad that harms children ' *The Daily Telegraph* 22 July 2010 [Online], Available: http://www.telegraph.co.uk/education/7905258/Special-needs-is-a-fad-that-harms-children.html

Glover, J. (1982) 'Letting people die' *London Review of Books* Vol. 4 No. 4, 4 March 1982 [Online], Available: http://www.lrb.co.uk/v04/n04/jonathan-glover/letting-people-die.

Goffman, E. (1990) *Stigma, Notes on the Management of Spoiled Identity*, London: Penguin.

Gould, S.J. (1984) *The Mismeasure of Man*, Harmondsworth:

Penguin Books Ltd.

Gove, M. (2008), 'We need a Swedish educational system' *The Independent* 3 December 2008 [Online], Available: http://www.independent.co.uk/opinion/commentators/michael-govewe-need-a-swedish-educationsystem-1048755.html.

Harmon, A. (2004) 'Burden of Knowledge: Tracking Prenatal Health; In New Tests for Fetal Defects, Agonizing Choices for Parents' *New York Times* 20 June 2004 [Online], Available: http://www.nytimes.com/2004/06/20/us/burden-knowledge-tracking-prenatal-health-new-tests-for-fetal-defects-agonizing.html?pagewanted=1.

Harris, R. and Andrews, T. (1988) 'Prenatal screening for Down's syndrome', *Archives of Disease in Childhood* vol. 63, no.7, pp.705-706.

Herrnstein, R.J. and Murray, C. (1994) *The Bell Curve, Intelligence and Class Structure in American Life,* New York: Simon & Schuster Inc.

HM Government (2010), *The Coalition: our programme for government* London: HM Government.

Hughes, S. (2009) *The Missing* Cambridge: Salt Publishing.

Huxley, A. (1977) *Brave New World,* London: HarperCollins Publishers.

James, S.D. (2009) 'Down Syndrome Births are down in the U.S.' *abc News* 2 November 2009 [Online], Available: http://abcnews.go.com/print?id=8960803 [accessed 24 June 2010].

Kuhse, H. and Singer, P. (1987) *Should the Baby Live? The Problem of Handicapped Infants,* Oxford: Oxford University Press.

Lamb, B. (2009), *Lamb Inquiry Special Educational Needs and Parental Confidence,* Nottingham: DCSF Publications, [Online], available: http://www.dcsf.gov.uk/lambinquiry/downloads/8553-lamb-inquiry.pdf.

Lawson, D. (2008) 'Shame on the doctors prejudiced against Down syndrome' *The Independent* 25th November 2008, [Online], Available: http://www.independent.co.uk/opinion/commentators/dominic-lawson/dominic-lawson-shame-on-the-doctors-prejudiced-against-down-syndrome-1033813.html [accessed 10 August 2010].

Loveys, K. (2010) 'Furious mother confronts comic Frankie Boyle over jokes about Down's syndrome victims' *Daily Mail* 9 April 2010.

Marrin, M. (2008) 'Parents of a Down's child must make painful choices' *The Sunday Times* 30 November 2008 [Online], Available: http://www.timesonline.co.uk/tol/comment/columnists/minette_marrin/article5258348.ece.

MENCAP (2007) *Death by Indifference, following up the Treat me right! Report* London: MENCAP.

Meyland-Smith, D. and Evans, N., (2009) *A Guide to School Choice Reforms*, London: Policy Exchange [Online], Available: http://www.policyexchange.org.uk/publications/publication.cgi?id=110.

Monckton, R. (2010) 'It makes my blood boil that so many normal children are deemed to have special needs' *Daily Mail* 29 July 2010 [Online], Available: http://www.dailymail.co.uk/femail/article-1298491/It-makes-blood-boil-normal-children-deemed-special-needs.html.

NDSCR, (2008) *The National Down Syndrome Cytogenetic Register 2006 Annual Report* London: NDSCR.

Newton, R. and Down's Syndrome Association (2004) *The Down's Syndrome Handbook: a practical guide for parents and carers*, London: Random House.

NHS, (2010) Antenatal Appointments – Screening Tests [Online], Available: http://www.nhs.uk/Conditions/Antenatal-screening

/Pages/When-should-it-be-done.aspx.

Ofcom (2010), *Audience attitudes towards offensive language on television and radio* London: Ofcom [Online], Available: http://stakeholders.ofcom.org.uk/binaries/research/tv-research/offensive-lang.pdf.

Pisa, N. (2010), 'Google executives convicted in Italy of violating privacy laws over bullying video', *The Daily Telegraph* 24 February 2010 [Online], Available: http://www.telegraph.co.uk/technology/google/7305616/Google-executives-convicted-in-Italy-of-violating-privacy-laws-over-bullying-video.html.

Quarmby, K. (2006) 'Inclusion debate treads new ground, are ministers pulling back from their resolves to educate all pupils in the mainstream?', *The Guardian*, 31 January 2006.

Quarmby, K. (2010) 'Freedom of expression, or a very modern freakshow?' *Index on Censorship Blog* 25 February 2010, [Online], Available: http://blog.indexoncensorship.org/2010/02/25/google-italy-disability-privacy/.

Ryan, J. and Thomas, F. (1987) *The Politics of Mental Handicap*, London: Free Association Books.

Scope, (2008) *Getting Away with Murder, Disabled people's experiences of hate crime in the UK*, London: Scope.

Select Committee on Education and Skills Third Report, (2006) Brief history of Special Educational Needs (SEN)' [Online], Available: http://www.publications.parliament.uk/pa/cm200506/cmselect/cmeduski/478/47805.htm.

Seyman, S. (2007), *People with Down's syndrome - Your Questions Answered* London: Down's Syndrome Association.

Shakespeare, T. (2008) 'Are we really more accepting of Down's syndrome?' *The Guardian* 24 November 2008 [Online], Available: http://www.guardian.co.uk/commentisfree/2008/nov/24/

disability-children.

Skotko, B. (2005) 'Mothers of Children with Down Syndrome Reflect on Their Postnatal Support' *Pediatrics* vol. 115, no. 1, January 2005, pp. 64-77.

Skotko, B.G. (2009) 'With new prenatal testing, will babies with Down syndrome slowly disappear', *Archives of Disease in Childhood* vol.94, no.11, pp.823-826.

Smith, S. (2010) '*Punching me in the face would have been preferable...*' [Online], Available: http://k1tt3ns.blogspot.com/2010/04/punching-me-in-face-would-have-been.html.

Sontag, S. (1991) *Illness as Metaphors and Aids and its Metaphors*, London: Penguin.

Taylor, S. (2004) 'The Right Not to Work, Power and Disability', *Monthly Review*, vol. 55, no. 10, March, pp.30-44.

The Commission on Special Needs in Education, (2007) *The Second Report of the Commission on Special Education Needs* London: The Conservative Party.

The Conservative Party (2009) *Big Society, Not Big Government* London: The Conservative Party.

Tickle, L. (2009) 'Should working with pupils with special educational needs be an essential part of teacher training?' *The Guardian*, 10 February 2009, [Online], available: http://www.guardian.co.uk/education/2009/feb/10/special-educational-needs.

Tizzard, J. (2002) ''Designer babies': the case for choice' in Lee, E (ed) *Debating Matters, where should we draw the line*, London: Hodder & Stoughton.

Tragester, C. (2010) 'Behind One Biotech's Meltdown' *Voice of San Diego* 6 July 2010 [Online], Available: http://www.voiceof-sandiego.org/science/article_2d12ed7e-8976-11df-aed1-001cc4c03286.html.

Tuckey, B. (2010) 'The boy in the corner: Why do children with special needs still get such a raw educational deal?', *The*

Independent, 11 April 2010.

UK National Screening Committee (NSC), (2008) *NHS Fetal Anomaly Screening Programme – Screening for Down's syndrome: UK NSC Policy recommendations 2007-2010: Model of Best Practice,* London: NSC.

United Nations *Declarations and Reservations* [Online], Available: http://www.un.org/disabilities/default.asp?id=475.

Walker, P. (2010) 'Frankie Boyle meets his match in mother of Down's syndrome child', *The Guardian* 8 April 2010.

Warnock, M. (2007) *Special Educational Needs: a new look* London: Philosophy of Education Society of Great Britain.

Warnock, M. and Norwich, B. (2010) *Special Educational Needs, a new look,* London: Continuum.

West, P. (2010) 'Frankie Boyle's Down's syndrome 'joke' was despicable – but we still need him' *The Telegraph* 9 April 2010 [Online], Available: http://blogs.telegraph.co.uk/culture/pwest/100007561/frankie-boyles-downs-syndrome-joke-was-despicable-but-we-still-need-him/comment-page-1/.

Wilkinson, E. (2010) 'Simple test could detect Down's', *BBC News* 30 June 2010 [Online], Available: http://www.bbc.co.uk/news/10453774.

Wright, O. and Frean, A. (2003) 'Down's screening for all mothers to be' *The Times,* 22 October 2003.

Žižek, S. (2009) *First as Tragedy, Then as Farce,* London: Verso.

Contemporary culture has eliminated both the concept of the public and the figure of the intellectual. Former public spaces – both physical and cultural – are now either derelict or colonized by advertising. A cretinous anti-intellectualism presides, cheerled by expensively educated hacks in the pay of multinational corporations who reassure their bored readers that there is no need to rouse themselves from their interpassive stupor. The informal censorship internalized and propagated by the cultural workers of late capitalism generates a banal conformity that the propaganda chiefs of Stalinism could only ever have dreamt of imposing. Zer0 Books knows that another kind of discourse – intellectual without being academic, popular without being populist – is not only possible: it is already flourishing, in the regions beyond the striplit malls of so-called mass media and the neurotically bureaucratic halls of the academy. Zer0 is committed to the idea of publishing as a making public of the intellectual. It is convinced that in the unthinking, blandly consensual culture in which we live, critical and engaged theoretical reflection is more important than ever before.